TOO BLESSED TO SAY YES

Praise for

TOO BLESSED TO SAY YES

"Jenny has written a timely book destined to align our hearts with a loving Father. Saying 'yes' to reading this book may be your first step to saying 'yes' to a God that wants immeasurably more for you than you could ever ask or imagine."

—Frank & Jessica Bealer
Family Pastors at Elevation Church

"In *Too Blessed to Say Yes*, Jenny has offered a timely and important counterpoint to the skewed view of blessing that is so common to our churches in America. The book is biblically faithful, theologically insightful and personally engaging. And it's funny. An excellent resource for both personal study and church discipleship. Highly recommended!"

—Ryan Lokkesmoe, PhD
Lead Pastor of Real Hope Community Church,
Author of *Blurry*

"In a passionate call for truth, Jenny challenges us to reevaluate the word 'blessing.' It seems blessings have become the ultimate pursuit, instead of pursuing the One who blesses. In a beautiful cascade of chapters, Jones shares how we can replace our inner need for comfort and material accolades with the freedom of maturity, as we redefine our pursuit of happiness. She's a stunning example of someone who has left a shallow understanding of faith for the deep waters of new hope and unbridled joy."

—Gari Meacham
Author of *Truly Fed, Spirit Hunger* and *Watershed Moments*
President of Truly Fed Ministries and The Vine Uganda

"Powerful story about a couple that wanted more out of life, and the steps they took to go after it. Written with wit and wisdom, Jenny will leave you feeling challenged and inspired at the same time. I could not put this book down!"

—Sue Miller
Live to Serve Champion at Orange
Author of *Making Your Children's Ministry the Best Hour of Every Kid's Week* and *Not Normal: 7 Quirks of Incredible Volunteers*

"What does 'blessing' really mean? Like so many words Christians use, this term has lost much of its power. Jenny Jones reminds us of what Scripture tells us blessing really looks like. Her timely and personal account is an inspiring reflection on where our true riches are found when we say 'yes' to the *best* things God offers us rather than the *good* things we so often think we need."

—Carey Nieuwhof
Founding Pastor of Connexus Church

"I met Jenny Jones about four years ago when she applied for my Infuse coaching/mentoring program. There were two things that made her stand out to me. First, she asked great questions. I love a person who asks great questions because that means they are lifetime learners. The second thing I soon learned about Jenny was that she wanted God's plans for her life more than anything else. I saw a person who was willing to 'walk out' obeying God and not just talk about it. I believe this book will do the same thing for all who read it-—it will help *you* desire to be a lifetime learner and help *you* desire God's plans for your life above your own. So what are you waiting on? Dig in and let Jenny's story impact your faith walk."

—Jim Wideman
Family Ministry Pioneer, Author
President of Jim Wideman Ministries

TOO BLESSED TO SAY YES

When the American Dream Keeps Us from Surrendering to God

JENNY DAY JONES

CLC PUBLICATIONS
Fort Washington, PA 19034

Too Blessed to Say Yes
Published by CLC Publications

U.S.A.
P.O. Box 1449, Fort Washington, PA 19034

UNITED KINGDOM
CLC International (UK)
Unit 5, Glendale Avenue, Sandycroft, Flintshire, CH5 2QP

Printed in the United States of America

ISBN (paperback): 978-1-61958-236-1
ISBN (e-book): 978-1-61958-237-8

Italics in Scripture quotations are the emphasis of the author.

Dedication

For Chad.
The way in which you sacrifice for God, our family and me is a daily illustration of the gospel to our little family. You are deeply loved because you deeply love. I am honored to be your wife and blessed to be your friend. I love you.

Contents

Foreword

Wendell Berry once wrote, "I am an ignorant pilgrim, crossing a dark valley. And yet for a long time, looking back, I have been unable to shake off the feeling that I have been led — make of that what you will."

Oftentimes it is difficult to see clearly or make sense of what is happening in our lives, especially in the midst of struggle or difficulty. It is only after (sometimes years after) that we are able to make any sense out of our journey at all.

I'm grateful for people like Jenny Jones who give us a map of their own pilgrimage of faith, renewing the possibility and hope that we are being led as well.

Reading *Too Blessed to Say Yes* is like getting a glimpse into Jenny's personal journal. She takes us on a journey that is honest, personal, challenging and beautiful.

In the following pages, you will journey with her in her search for an authentic expression of faith that goes beyond a "checklist," performance-oriented Christianity.

She describes a growing restlessness and discontent with an American-branded form of faith, which defines "blessed" as something that is rooted only in personal benefit. But she doesn't get stuck in a cynical, church-bashing trap like so many others. Instead, she unpacks, with biblical and personal stories, what “blessed” really means.

Jenny, who is wonderfully flawed like us, shares her own crisis of faith and turning point (which she describes as a “rich-young-ruler moment”), where she began to move from the pursuit of “the American dream” to a relentless pursuit of the dream of God. A dream of a people who “reflect a life that is poor in spirit, meek, righteous, merciful, pure in heart and peaceful.” A dream of a kingdom that has less to do with us and more to do with the poor, oppressed, fatherless and the hungry.

In doing so, she tackles issues like fear of failure, performance Christianity, radical generosity and risk-taking. She challenges us to continually and deliberately empty ourselves and “say ‘yes’ to God.”

Like Joseph of Arimithea and Zacchaeus, Jenny shows that saying “yes” means life will never be the same again. And that is a good thing. It's not always “rainbows and unicorns” as Jenny clearly points out . . . but ALWAYS worth it.

I’ve never been one to live my life in order to “keep up with the Joneses." But in looking at the example of Jenny and her husband, Chad . . . that wouldn’t be such a bad thing.

Rob Morris
President & Cofounder of Love146

Acknowledgments

Ryland, Seth, Wyatt and Kennedy—being your mom is the greatest privilege of my entire life. Thank you for your patience, unconditional love, contagious joy and laughter. You each serve our family and our community in ways that represent Christ so well, and I am so incredibly proud of you. I pray that you always follow Jesus with all your heart, even when it doesn't make sense to anyone else around you!

Mike and Pam Day (aka Mom and Dad)—the fact that I am writing an acknowledgments page at all is due to both of you! Thank you for never ever telling me I couldn't do something (even when it was painfully obvious that I couldn't), because that foundation has always pushed me just enough over the edge at just the moments I needed it—like when I was writing the pages of this book! No one else on this earth has cheered, supported and prayed for me like the two of you have. I'm thankful God thought you two could handle a daughter like me!

Lon and Kathy Jones—first off, thank you for raising such an amazing son that has turned out to be the best husband and daddy I could ever have hoped for—most if not all of that is attributed to you. Second, thank you for the countless times you have driven back and forth from Austin to Houston to be present in the lives of your grandchildren and to help their momma pursue all that God is calling her to do! This book would not have happened without the numerous times you swooped in to save the day for the Jones' kids (and me too)!

Ryan and Ashley Lokkesmoe—thank you both for believing in me on a personal level and, now, on a professional level. Thank you for stepping out in faith to start Real Hope. There is not another family Chad and I could imagine riding this roller coaster called "church planting" with. We have so much respect for both of you and can't wait to see how God is going to use this little church of ours to radically impact the world! Ryan, thank you for connecting me with CLC and for answering all the millions of questions I have had throughout this entire process—this book literally would not exist had you not thought of me in that one conversation! Ashley, thank you for the many tears we have shed together and the way in which you always honor God with your actions. I am too stubborn to follow the leadership of many, but it is an honor to follow the two of you.

Sue Miller—thank you for being hands down the most encouraging person I have ever met! For the past several years, you have challenged me and made me ask myself some really hard questions; but even in that you have this amazing ability to speak into the potential you see in me, not what is happening right then. Thank you for going out on a limb that one day and telling me that you thought I would be a great executive pastor—I sure hope you're right!

Melysa, Jen, Leslie, Mel, Joy and Rachel (aka the Squad)—there is not another group on this planet who is more excited to see this book in print, mostly because now I will stop talking about it! Thank you for not letting me quit and for reading so much of this book in its raw, unedited form and still believing that it was good! Thank you for walking beside me through not only the ups and downs of this book, but also through life! You ladies tell it like it is and then pray for it to be different! You love Jesus with all your heart and pursue Him passionately. I love doing life with you all!

Real Hope Community Church—thank you for saying "yes" to something so new, so organic and still so unknown. By the time this book is released, we will have had our first service (barely), but so many of you joined this community before any service had ever occurred. When you said "yes," there were no fancy worship centers, no themed kids' or students' areas—in fact, there is still no building at all—just God's vision for a group of people to impact a community with the "Real Hope" of Jesus Christ. Thank you for saying "yes" when you did and for every day to come.

Becky English and the staff at CLC—first to Becky, thank you for not allowing me to sound like a complete idiot! You are so talented at what you do, and I am so thankful to have had you working on this project. The way in which you were able to work through and communicate the passion behind this book as if it was your own was astounding. Thank you for loving and respecting my story the way you did—I will be forever grateful for your fingerprints on this book. Erika Cobb, Dave Almack, and the other staff at CLC—thank you for taking a risk on a no-name author and giving me a platform in which to communicate my love for Jesus and His Word. I will always hold dear the ability to say that I am a CLC author.

1

When Did Christianity Get So Boring?

I love a good list. I'm talking about a well-thought-out, boxes-just-waiting-to-be-checked kind of list—one that I can see at the end of the day and use to size up my self-worth based on its completion. For as long as I can remember, I have started every project with a solid checklist. Little did I know that my penchant for lists would one day result in a spiritual crisis that would forever change my life.

Last year my family did a checklist experiment. To try and keep our small army of children from getting expelled from school and their mother from losing her job due to perpetual tardiness, my husband and I made each kid various checklists to aid them as they got ready for school in the morning. (Okay, I confess, not just for the morning—we made a when-you-get-home-from-school checklist, a before-you-touch-any-form-of-electronics checklist, a before-you-go-to-bed checklist, a when-you-wake-up-in-the-morning checklist, a try-all-these-possible-options-before-asking-Mom checklist.) I kid you not; the closest I have ever been to actual warfare in my entire life is between six thirty and quarter after seven each morning in the Jones household. Getting four children under the age of ten out the door at any time of day is quite the feat, but doing it in the morning—when I have to get them to three different schools with multiple backpacks, folders, lunch boxes, snacks, nap mats, "All About Me" posters and shoes on their feet—is no joke!

But I'll tell you what—those lists work; before my husband and I even said the word "reward," my kids were already asking what they were going to get for completing their lists. We have been trained to think that a completed list produces a reward. After a week of my kids completing the lists, they got snow cones; after a semester, they got a weekend trip with Mom and Dad; after an entire school year, they got a cat (yes, a real live cat).

Lists can be exciting (that isn't sarcasm—I am dead serious)! They can show us where we have been and where we still need to go. They can help us make a plan, stick to a deadline, and flat out get things done.

But despite their amazing benefits, lists can also turn a person into a hard-driving, relationally inept taskmaster (or so I've been told). I would eventually figure this out for myself when I became my own worst taskmaster.

Giving My All for God

When I was growing up, I did not take long to realize the power of a well-crafted checklist. In fact, when I was twelve years old, I started a checklist for the largest project I would ever attempt to tackle—the checklist for my life.

Now before you get too excited, I should be totally transparent. My story is not one of intrigue, betrayal or drug addictions; in fact, it is pretty average at best. It actually looks very much like most of the people I have met, live close to and go to church with. I have lived in the same suburban city outside Houston, Texas my entire life. I'm not famous in the grand scheme of history; I am just another face in the crowd. But during the summer between my sixth- and seventh- grade years, I felt what it was like to be truly known for the very first time.

Like most girls in middle school, I desperately wanted to be liked by my peers, and I was willing to do just about anything to be accepted. Every day I worked hard to look as if I had just walked off the set of *Dawson's Creek* (television series) in my flannel print skirt and chunky Mary Jane shoes.

I joined every club, sports team and school activity I could think of and made sure I was the right person for whatever group of people I was with at the time. I was shallow and fake. I was a sixth-grade girl. But in spite of my high aspirations to write the perfect entry in all of my friendship journals, God used my desire to be popular and known to draw me to Him—even at twelve years old—and He did it through a school locker!

In junior high, each of us was issued a locker in order to house our necessities—our backpacks, textbooks, pictures of friends, 'N Sync posters, Axe body spray, Dr. Pepper-flavored lip smackers—you know, the essentials. That year, as the Lord would have it, Katy Junior High was over capacity, and every locker had two students assigned to it.

This led to the most pressing question of my life in 1996: With whom would I share a locker? I mean, this was the person I would be seen with in the halls, possibly associated with, and, at the very least, would have to talk to on a regular basis—the stuff that makes or breaks a kid's first shot at any sort of reputation in the sixth grade.

By divine appointment, I now know, I was paired up with the daughter of the chairman of deacons at the local First Baptist Church. At the time this felt like a fatal blow to my bid for reign as most popular sixth grader ever; but it turned out that the church girl was pretty popular (as is the case in most small towns in Texas) and, therefore, so was I by default.

Sheryl and I quickly became best friends, and eventually I found myself at her house most weekends. In the Dauchy household, however, there was a strict policy of no Saturday night sleepovers unless guests go to church on Sunday. That's just the way it was. Because of that one rule, the course of my life was forever changed.

Before I walked into the doors of First Baptist Church in Katy, Texas, I knew nothing about Jesus. My family was more of an attend-church-on-Christmas-and-Easter type of family. But now, as I started learning about Jesus, I became hooked. The incarnation of Christ fascinated me.

As a sixth grader, I didn't know the word "incarnation" or what it meant, but I could not get over the fact that the very Son of God would leave the most perfect place ever created to die for me. And for what? What had I ever done for Him?

It was mind blowing to me that anyone would give his life for me. In that moment in the sixth grade, when I recognized God's grace, I decided that I would tirelessly run after Jesus for the rest of my life, because the only way I knew to thank Him was to give Him my life.

My love for God led to a checklist of items that I wanted to do for Him. I was going to change the world! But in all my planning what I did not pick up on was the fact that only one Person is capable of changing the world, and it isn't Jenny Jones. But I sure was going to try—for Jesus, of course. After all, He needed me. Over the next sixteen years I checked off a pretty impressive list of accomplishments:

- ☑ Be the poster child of my youth group. Check.
- ☑ Don't make the same mistakes that my brothers made. Check.
- ☑ Be a good, easy kid for my parents to raise. Check.
- ☑ Commit my life to full-time ministry. Check.
- ☑ Don't get involved in sex, drugs or rock 'n' roll. Check.
- ☑ Marry the perfect guy. Check.
- ☑ Have awesome kids. Check.
- ☑ Be a pastor. Check.
- ☑ Be a pastor at a megachurch. Check.
- ☑ Be debt free. Check.
- ☑ Be financially smart. Check.
- ☑ Buy a house. Check.
- ☑ Buy a better house. Check.
- ☑ Help the orphaned, widowed and poor. Check.

The list could go on and on. My pursuit, however, unhealthily fed my extremely competitive and addictive personality. This kind of personality is not always a bad thing—in fact, it has come in handy for me many times, like when I graduated from college, powered through a series on Netflix, or discovered a newfound addiction to CrossFit. But over the years, this characteristic had quite an adverse affect on my spiritual life.

Though none of the items on my list were bad, somewhere along the way the list stopped being about Jesus and started being about me. My "yes" to Jesus slowly turned into saying "yes" to myself. My list stopped being freeing and started becoming suffocating. It stopped building in me a surrendered heart to what God had called me to do and started building in me a heart that was driven by attention, recognition and doting words. The worst part? I had used God as the reason to gain it all.

A Checklist—or a Surrendered Heart?

You see, when I created my checklist, I was unintentionally defining Jesus' plan for me. I began to lean on my own understanding and to believe that my ways were better than His ways. In an effort to always *do* for Him, I ran the risk of developing an attitude of selfishness and arrogance. Instead of having a surrendered heart, I developed agendas and goals.

I did not live for Jesus, but for my dreams and for myself. I didn't realize it at the time, but my attention had turned to possessions, bank accounts and maintaining a social status to fit my middle-class suburban community. I became *too blessed to say yes.*

An illustration of this can be found in Luke 10:38–42. "As Jesus and his disciples were on their way, he came to a village where a woman named Martha opened her home to him" (10:38). So far, so good for Martha. "She had a sister called Mary, who sat at the Lord's feet listening to what he said. But Martha was distracted by all the preparations that had to be made. She came to him and asked, 'Lord, don't you care that my sister has left me to do the work by myself? Tell her to help me!'" (10:39–40).

But Jesus had some corrective words for Martha and her checklist. "'Martha, Martha,' the Lord answered, 'you are worried and upset about many things, but few things are needed—or indeed only one. Mary has chosen what is better, and it will not be taken away from her'" (10:41–42).

Now I have to be honest. I have always felt that Martha gets a bad rap here. I know how frantically I clean my house and threaten my children not to touch a thing or get out a single toy when guests are coming over (whether it's someone I want to impress or not), so just imagine how you would act if Jesus—the very *Son of God*—was coming for a dinner party. You would be a crazy person too!

But this resulted in Martha missing a chance to get to know and spend time with Jesus, because she had not surrendered her own plans and priorities to Christ. Her checklist was not necessarily bad, but it wasn't what Christ wanted for her in that moment; it was what she wanted.

I see so much of myself in Martha. Mary, on the other hand, was surrendered at the feet of Jesus. Not only did she make the better choice, but Jesus said it would not be taken away from her. Jesus wanted Martha to experience the blessing that comes with completely surrendering herself to knowing Him.

Essentially, Jesus said to her, "Martha, you have this agenda that you think is so important, but you are so caught up in it that it has become about you. Only one thing mattered tonight—that you spend time worshiping Me." Just as Martha's checklist could not bring her closer to Jesus, neither can our checklists bring us closer to Him. We can only really know Jesus when we surrender our hearts.

Reality Check

Fast-forward sixteen years from that day in sixth grade when I accepted Christ. I had gone from that twelve-year-old little girl desperately searching for significance to a twenty-eight-year-old woman searching once again and getting very weary from the journey. I had every blessing a person could want—the world's best husband, three amazing kids, a beautiful house, a great job and money in the bank. But in all honesty, I had become bored with life. Years of serving God on my own terms and being sidetracked by the American dream[1] had led me to a point of spiritual crisis.

One particularly weary night in July 2013, I sat on our couch and looked at my husband, Chad, and simply said, "If this is all that Christianity is about—doing the right thing, checking the right boxes—then I'm out. I can't keep trying to pursue the next best thing. I have done everything I'm supposed to do the way I'm supposed to do it, and I have never felt more tired and empty. When did Christianity get so boring? When did it stop being enough?"

At this time, I was on staff at one of the fastest-growing churches in America. I was leading a ministry of more than 750 kids and 400 volunteers, and I sat on our church's elder team and senior leadership team.

Despite all this, I knew very few Christians who resembled those in the New Testament—myself included. I am not talking metaphorically, I mean literally. I did not know a lot of people, or maybe any people, who had ever actually sold everything they had and given it to the poor (see Luke 18:22) or chosen to live communally (see Acts 4:32–35) or relied on the Lord for everything without worry (see Matt. 6:25) or intentionally found self-sacrificing ways to love their neighbor as themselves (see Mark 12:31) or had widows and orphans living with them (see James 1:27).

I could not shake the fact that, after professing to be an active, growing Christian for sixteen years, not only did my life not reflect the life of Christ's followers in the New Testament, it didn't look too different from that of anyone else in my community. So on that night in July, I made one last deal with God: I told Him that as a last-ditch effort, I would read through the entire New Testament. I would try to do so as if I had never read it before, and I would take Jesus at His word. I would not have any preconceived notions—it would just be my Bible, the Holy Spirit and me.

This was quite the challenge as I had been a biblical studies major and had pretty much lived and breathed fun classes like biblical exegesis of the New Testament for four years of my life (okay, fine, five!). That night I even made the commitment to God that if He showed Himself to me in an authentic way, I would do anything He asked.

A Different Kind of "Blessed"

During the next six months, God met me in such a way that my life was completely turned upside down. As I read, I began to notice that Jesus really had only two concerns: building the kingdom of God and loving people, particularly those in need. And He talked about those two things a lot—like nonstop.

Jesus was more concerned with relationships than with rules, and I began to see that a lot of the people who Jesus spent time with had a different definition of "blessed" than I did.

Most of these individuals had very little in terms of money or material possessions, but they gave freely what they did have. And what they lacked in resources, they more than made up for in their gigantic kind of faith. Jesus' disciples weren't showy or famous—outside of their families they were unknown and ordinary.

They strived for excellence, but not so they could get to the top of the corporate ladder or post pictures of their new rides on

Instagram and hashtag them "#blessed." They left family members, served food and washed feet (sometimes even with their tears); they were kicked out of towns, beaten and even killed.

They were persecuted in ways unlike anything you and I have experienced in today's world. Their lives weren't blessed as a result of what they owned or obtained; rather, their lives were blessed as a result of what they gave away.

I can say with complete sincerity that I have never experienced a time in which I have learned more about who Jesus is, sought more fervently after the Holy Spirit and consumed more words of the Bible than I did in that six-month period of reading the New Testament. I was like someone starving to death. And in my hunger God met me.

Chad was reading through the New Testament during this season as well, and every night we talked about what we were reading. He was not having the same depth of struggle that I was, but he agreed with me that we had gotten off-kilter in our perspective of blessing, and he was open to whatever the Lord would have for our lives.

As we both read, Chad and I came to the conclusion that we were done—done with the status quo, done with the so-called American dream. We were done with serving others only when it was convenient, made sense or, dare I say, produced warm and fuzzy feelings inside of us. We were done with saying that we modeled our lives after Christ when we actually lived lives that looked more like suburbia than the New Testament.

Our lives up to this point had seemed less about having surrendered hearts toward God and more about the stuff we possessed, the neighborhood we lived in, the schools our kids went to and how much money something would cost us—things that at the end of the day didn't really matter. As we faced the reality that we needed to change our perspective, we had to repent of our misplaced priorities and put God first in our lives in new ways. Yes, we had both repented of our sins when we had first chosen to follow Jesus, but now we experienced a further repentance that would lead to spiritual growth and maturity—a surrendering of our rights and plans to God both inwardly and outwardly.

We found it ironic that the very things we had called blessings in our lives were the very things that had held us back from saying "yes" to what God wanted for us! We decided that we were done with such concerns as: *But we might have to move! What if we can't afford that? Will that mean a pay cut? We don't have room in our house to do that!*

It was time to stop overvaluing what we considered blessings and to say "yes" to the bigger plan God had for us. Something clicked, and all of a sudden nothing made sense except two things: building the kingdom of God and loving people.

Testing Our Resolve

I wish the story ended there, but in that six-month period of revolution in our lives, I also experienced more sadness, uncertainty and overall confusion than I ever had before. Just a few short weeks into our newfound sense of purpose, my mom was told that her pesky cough was an extremely aggressive form of lung cancer—a type that statistically spreads to other places in the body 80 percent of the time.

I am the third child in my family and the only girl. My mom lived five minutes from my house and worked full-time at our church, where I also worked. I saw her almost every single day and never lived more than twenty minutes away from her during twenty-nine of my thirty-one years of life. To say that my mom and I were close and that this diagnosis was devastating to me was an understatement.

I found myself in survival mode. My family took things one day at a time, because that was all we could do. We could not think past the moment right in front of us. To try and think about the future was just too hard. But even in this crisis, Chad and I stayed the course of our commitment to build the kingdom of God and to love people.

My parents didn't really know all that Chad and I were thinking about, but they too were holding on to God in the midst of this trial. While my mom received treatment, my dad told other patients about Jesus' saving grace. In the thick of chemo and radiation, my mom fervently prayed for healing for others who were also fighting cancer.

I can't tell you that I didn't worry that my mom might die, because I did; or that in the middle of explaining cancer to my two-, five- and seven-year-olds, I didn't have to excuse myself and let my husband finish the conversation since I couldn't control my emotions for even one more second, because I did; or that I didn't ask God on a daily basis why this had to be part of our story, because I did. I did all those things. But as we continued to say "yes" to God and "no" to ourselves, God was faithful to meet us every day in His Word and through other people.

Putting Our "Yes" into Action

One of the beautiful things God did during this time was to open Chad's and my eyes to the plight of orphans around the world, and we quickly knew that we needed to play a role in helping these children in some way. It's sad to say that up until this point, the most exposure I had to orphans was from the movie *Annie*. We started out by researching how we could financially support orphans—you know, send them or their orphanage money. We quickly found a great organization that allowed us to sponsor kids who were in danger of becoming poverty orphans (i.e., children whose parents can no longer provide for them due to poverty). We sponsored a couple of kids. We felt pretty good about that and checked it off the list. But God reminded us that checklists are not His preferred method of building His kingdom and loving people.

Recall that I had made a deal with God that if He were to authentically reveal Himself to me through His Word, I would say "yes" to whatever He asked me to do. Chad, too, was listening for God's guidance, and the two of us were ready to make any changes that the Lord wanted us to make in our lives.

Well, as it turns out, there is a pretty explicit verse in the New Testament regarding orphans: "Religion that God our Father accepts as pure and faultless is this: to look after orphans and widows in their distress and to keep oneself from being polluted by the world" (James 1:27). Quite clearly, God was trying to get Chad's and my attention.

We reminded God, however, that He had already given us three precious rays of sunshine. But He gently reminded us that we had already said "yes" and that He was keenly aware of how many children we had. Touché. So Chad and I began researching adoption. We made it clear to God, however, that we were not going to take any action on this new idea for at least a year.

One night after I had just fallen asleep, our then two-year-old, Wyatt, woke up crying. I got out of bed and climbed the stairs (while having a very impassioned inner dialogue about the facts that my husband was sound asleep in bed, and Wyatt seemed to have no regard for the reality that I had to wake up for work in just a few hours).

When I got to my son's room, he was sitting up in bed crying. So I went to him, got him to lay down and started singing his favorite song at the time, "The Wheels on the Bus." (I know, we are really deep with our bedtime songs—don't be jealous.)

As I stroked his hair and watched him fall back asleep, tears started streaming down my face. Not just a few tears—a floodgate was released. It took all I had to choke out "all through the town." In that moment all I could see was a little girl in an orphanage waking up crying in the middle of the night with no one to sing "The Wheels on the Bus" to her or stroke her hair, and *it unraveled me*.

I began crying so uncontrollably that I had to leave the room so I wouldn't reawaken my son. I went downstairs and sat on the couch, and the Holy Spirit immediately laid it on my heart to pray for our future daughter—for her safety, health, development and security—because she was alive right then and needed us now, not in a year! So I did. I spent the rest of the night praying; you don't go back to sleep after something like that! The next day I told Chad what had happened, and he responded, "Then we will start the process today." And we did.

As my mom sat in a chair having chemo pumped into her body, I told her about her next grandchild. And fifteen months later, on March 9, 2015, in the city of Taiyuan in the Shanxi province of the People's Republic of China, we welcomed Kennedy Elaine Jones into our family. Coming to the end of myself and ditching my checklist had changed our lives forever.

Chad and Jenny Jones with their newly adopted daughter, Kennedy.

Letting God Change Our Stories

As I think back to how my story started off, with a twelve-year-old girl who hopelessly needed a Savior and a Father who loved her wildly enough to offer her His Son, I am taken aback by how gradually (almost unnoticeably) my journey turned from pursuing Christ to pursuing what our culture would call a blessed life.

I spent sixteen years chasing my own plans and desires, and in so doing, I put God in a box that didn't amount to much more than a well-intentioned checklist. To the outside world I had a great career, an amazing family, supportive friends and a beautiful home; for all intents and purposes, my life appeared to be the exact definition of blessed.

But I had aligned my life with those around me instead of with God's Word, and I had ended up off course and far from truth.

I wish I knew your story—how far you have come in your journey with Christ, how far you still desire to go. I wish I could sit across from you at First Cup Café (my favorite local coffee shop) and dive into talking about what you still need to surrender—what checklist you have formed that defines your definition of a blessed life and how you got to that conclusion.

I don't know what God is asking you to surrender right now; but I do know that our God is a jealous God, and He desires to know us so much so that sometimes He just may bring us to a place of surrender even if we don't ask for it.

One thing I have learned: the preemptive strike of voluntary surrender is always less painful than being shaken up by God as He attempts to get our attention.

It is time that we, as followers of Christ, stop living mundane stories that look like everyone else's. The God who transformed Peter, Paul, Zacchaeus and Matthew (just to name a few) is not out of business.

Now more than ever He is looking for those who will not be boxed in by what society says is a blessed and successful life but, rather, are more concerned with having a heart of obedience than a house full of stuff. He is looking for those who will say "yes" to Him before He even asks—no matter the sacrifice.

I am thankful that God was faithful to intervene in my life. Isn't it just like Him to take our narrow and shallow definition of walking with Him and shatter it with something we could never have imagined possible? My prayer is that those of us who are believers in Jesus Christ will rethink our way of life as we have known it and begin to imagine, dream and allow God to paint a picture of what could be and should be in each of our lives.

Don't be too blessed to say "yes" to God.

2

But Your Love Doesn't Pay My Bills

We love sentiments like "The best things in life are free—hugs, smiles, friends, kisses, family, sleep, love, laughter, good memories." (That's precious. It's an anonymous quote, so go ahead and pin or Instagram or tweet or post to whatever your social-media fancy may be—just be sure to hashtag it "#blessed." Okay, I'm joking. Don't do that.)

But even while we smile pleasantly at the idea that hugs, friends and laughter constitute the best things in life, our internal thought process is really more in alignment with the lyrics to the 1959 song "Money (That's What I Want)."

> The best things in life are free
> But you can give them to the birds and bees
> I need money (that's what I want) . . .
> Your love give me such a thrill
> But your love don't pay my bills
> I need money (that's what I want) . . .
> Money don't get everything, it's true
> But what it don't get, I can't use

> I need money (that's what I want) . . .
> Always need greens (that's what I want) [1]

My favorite line is "Your love give me such a thrill, but your love don't pay my bills." And for some of us American believers, this is our mind-set toward God when it comes to our finances.

We might not say it out loud, because it's not very Christian, but the way we manage our finances is an extension of our hearts. And when we refuse to line up our finances with what is important to the heart of God, it points to deeper issues of control and a lack of faith. In other words, we don't trust God with our stuff—and with our lives.

In the months following my spiritual crisis and Chad's and my "yes" to God, I began to wonder if there were other people like me, who were bored and stagnant in their Christian lives, who were tired of checklists and hungry for more than a complacent Christian existence. I began to realize that maybe we weren't the only Christians caught up in the *blessing* of the American dream, that the problem might be endemic among churches in the Western world.

Perhaps this is why Paul wrote in First Timothy 6:10, "The love of money is a root of all kinds of evil. Some people, eager for money, have wandered from the faith and pierced themselves with many griefs." Now wealth in and of itself does not cause believers to "wander from the faith," because financial resources, when used to promote the two most important things to Jesus—building the kingdom of God and loving people—can be transformational.

But Paul was warning Timothy about the danger of being discontented, which can lead to greed and to missing God's plan for our lives. Paul had seen both new and seasoned believers walk away from their faith because of greed, and he had seen the "many griefs" that had followed. The love of money caused Judas to hand Jesus over to the chief priests (see Luke 22:1–6) and Ananias and Sapphira to lose their lives (see Acts 5:1–11).

Ultimately, though, the real problem with loving money is that it distracts us from a single-minded pursuit of God. It causes us to put our faith and security in something tangible instead of in the One who created tangible things. And it causes us to confuse our identity in our relationship with God—we begin to view ourselves as owners rather than stewards. After all, we worked hard for what we have!

But everything we have is a gift from God, and the sooner we recognize His ownership over our possessions and our lives, the sooner we will find ourselves on the way to a blessed life.

A Steward's Responsibility

My ten-year-old daughter, Ryland, is very much into earning money right now. Well, let me clarify—she is very much into *buying* things; and because our household works very much like a benevolent dictatorship, she has to work to support her personal interests.

A while back she came to me and asked for a list of tasks she could do to earn money on a more consistent basis. After a few months she had racked up quite a bit of capital and was ready to cash in her earnings. I took her to the store, and you know what she wanted to buy? Play-Doh.

I went into a rant right in the middle of Toys "R" Us about being wise with money and spending it on something useful, blah-blah-blah. "What's the big deal?" you ask. "Let the kid spend her money on Play-Doh if she wants to!"

Here's the big deal: If you walked into our game room, you would see a bin the size of my three-year-old just full of Play-Doh. Neon colors, primary colors, glitter colors, glow in the dark—you name it, we have it! The Jones family should buy stock in Play-Doh.

But here's the bigger issue: Where did my ten-year-old get all of her spending money? From her parents. Did she earn it? Yes. Was it fully in her possession? Yes. But ultimately it had come from her parents (the owners) and had been transferred to her (the steward), and therefore the thought of her deciding (as a steward does) to spend the money on something she already had no less than seventy-five containers of . . . well, let's just say that it did not sit well with me.

God must have the same reaction to our spending choices at times. He gives us opportunities to earn money, which ultimately He has provided, and then watches us spend our earnings on meaningless things that do nothing to further His kingdom or love people.

After some intense conversation in the middle of Toys "R" Us, I figured out that Ryland (who is über-crafty—a trait she didn't get from her mama) just wanted something she could create. Eventually she settled on a Rainbow Loom (Google it if you aren't familiar with it; then buy one for any kid you have even the most remote interest in, and thank me later).

Fast-forward a few months, and Ryland and her best friend used their Rainbow Looms to make and sell bracelets—and they used the profits to help purchase a cow through World Vision for a family in Uganda. Yes, I said a *cow*!

That cow would provide milk for the family to sell, the ability to transport goods and an opportunity to breed more cattle in the future—an economic game changer for this family. Now *that* made her mom happy.

A steward is responsible for deciding how to spend his owner's money—and as believers, we are stewards of what God has given us, not owners.

We can spend the owner's money on something excessive or self-serving (Play-Doh), or we can use our gifts and spend our financial resources on something we love to do that can also benefit others (Rainbow Loom). When we seek God and ask Him how we can make the latter a reality, our stewardship decisions build the kingdom of God and love people.

How do we figure out how to best use God's money? Well, I don't mean to be all cliché or to give a cop-out answer, but we have an entire book that does a great job of telling us how to honor God in every area of our lives—finances included. That book is the Bible.

If we want to follow Christ, at some point we have to decide to align our lives with the Bible and not expect the Bible to align itself with our lives.

And there it is, folks—it only took me until chapter 2 to start talking about money! Maybe you are thinking, *Man, I can't wait to feel uncomfortable for the next 150 or so pages!* But Paul's warning to Timothy about the "love of money" was not just a first-century stronghold isolated to the crowd to whom Timothy was ministering.

Greed has a grip on our lives and society in the twenty-first century, particularly in the United States—and if we want to shake off this grip, getting a little uncomfortable may not be such a bad thing.

How the American Dream Has Distorted the Gospel

Money is an inanimate object; it does not have a heart, breath or feelings. Money gains power only when it is tied to an emotion, which means that people are the only ones who can give money power.

Humans can use money to change someone's entire future by offering them food, clothes, clean water and an opportunity for an education; or we can use it to purchase other human beings like some commodity, build weapons of mass destruction, supply addictions and ruin families. What we empower with our money depends on our motives.

Dictionary.com defines the American dream as "a life of personal happiness and material comfort as traditionally sought by individuals in the U.S."[2] Americans today have more open doors to education, health care, jobs and transportation than ever before. Yet here's our problem: we aren't stewarding our opportunities well. The gap between the wealthy and the poor is becoming wider and wider, and the number of people willing to give resources to bridge that gap is becoming smaller and smaller.

This isn't just my maybe-too-liberal, millennial opinion—it is fact. *The Chronicle of Philanthropy* website features an interactive map called "How America Gives."[3] On this map a person can search areas of the country by zip code and compare the percentage of charitable giving to the average gross income of a household.

I live in the fastest-growing zip code in the United States.[4] Our growth rate is mainly attributed to the oil industry, so our community has developed a fairly high standard of living that has changed what is considered normal. Some of the many perks of living in our zip code are the great schools, amazing houses and booming economy—the perfect formula for any family trying to achieve the American dream.

So naturally I searched my zip code on the "How America Gives" map, and what I found was astounding. According to this site, the more money a family in my community makes, the less (in terms of percentage) they give.

A family that makes up to $25,000 annually gives 8.25 percent with an average contribution of $2,164 a year, while a family that makes $200,000 or more annually gives 1.89 percent with an average contribution of $8,772 dollars a year.

To my type A brain this made no sense. The more we make, the more we should give, right? But that is not what is happening—not in my community anyway—and I would venture to say that it probably isn't happening in yours either.

Now you may be thinking, *Okay, but the research you listed referred to Americans in general. What about Americans who define themselves as Christians?* Well, according to *Relevant* magazine, "Christians are only giving at 2.5 percent per capita, while during the Great Depression they gave at a 3.3 percent rate."[5] Christians give less now than they did during the worst economic period in our country's history.

I observe the stronghold of this American dream mind-set almost daily in my community, my church and, at times, even my own family.

Getting the better house, driving the nicer car, taking more vacations, getting our kids on the right teams, moving up the corporate ladder and retiring on a golf course have become the end goals for many of us. If we can achieve all that, or even half of it, we consider ourselves blessed.

So the big question is, why? Why, when we make more, do we give less? Why, despite having moved up the economic ladder, is the percentage of our giving sliding down? The answer is not that complex: we have put the quest for the American dream over the pursuit of God and generosity.

And the scary thing is, we may not even know the grip it has on us—to the extent that we honestly believe that running after the American dream *is* running after God! After all, doesn't God want us to provide for our families?

Of course He does—but He also wants us to trust Him and to use what He's given us for the work of the gospel and the help of others. Let's look at four reasons why it is so hard for us to be generous as we climb the economic ladder.

Reason 1: The More We Make, the More We Want

The saying goes, "The numbers don't lie." And that's true—except when it comes to giving. Remember, a family in my community in the "up to $25,000" bracket gives 8.25 percent with an average contribution of $2,164 a year, while a family in the "$200,000 or more" bracket gives 1.89 percent with an average contribution of $8,772 a year. While the differences are 6.36 percent in favor of the lower income brackets, the actual dollar amount given is a difference of $6,608 in favor of the higher income bracket.

My point is, we only see the bottom line. We say to ourselves, *This year we gave close to $7,000 more than we gave last year, so of course we're giving more—the numbers don't lie.* One of the best biblical illustrations to correct this line of thinking can be found in Luke 21:1–4.

> As Jesus looked up, he saw the rich putting their gifts into the temple treasury. He also saw a poor widow put in two very small copper coins. "Truly I tell you," he said, "this poor widow has put in more than all the others. All these people gave their gifts out of their wealth; but she out of her poverty put in all she had to live on." (Luke 21:1–4)

To put this into a modern-day perspective, the widow gave away about two dollars.[6] Though many people walked into the temple and gave much larger amounts, their tithing was not sacrificial in any way—they were giving "out of their wealth; but she out of her poverty."

One of my favorite quotes on the subject of giving is by author and pastor Mark Batterson. He says, "When God blesses you financially, don't raise your *standard of living*. Raise your *standard of giving*."[7] The reason a quote like that is such a kick in the pants to us is because it is so foreign to how many of us were raised.

We've been taught to think that we work more to earn more to get more. But this is the exact opposite of what the early believers did: "They sold property and possessions to give to anyone who had need" (Acts 2:45).

A year ago, Chad and I did something that I am confident made my extended family believe more than ever before that we had lost our ever-lovin' minds! We sat down and had a real conversation about what it takes to provide for the needs of our family of six. (Notice I said needs, not wants.) After we got that number, we decided that everything past that number we would give away. We refused to work more just so we could get more.

In the wake of this decision, a week before my performance evaluation at work (when my salary is always set for the next year), I went into my pastor's office and told him that I was not interested in a raise for the coming year.

This was a risky move—not just from a financial standpoint but from an egotistical one. I basically communicated, "I clearly killed it last year and know that in return you are going to want to throw money at me; however, I'm so above reproach that I have to say 'no.'"

Needless to say, I had to tread lightly. (Come to think of it, I might have the worst self-awareness ever and really did my boss a favor by avoiding a truly uncomfortable conversation. Either way, ignorance is bliss, right?)

My pastor looked at me and simply responded, "Okay, I need to think about this for a minute. I have honestly never had anyone say this to me before." I don't tell you this story to give the impression that I walk around every day looking for ways to be as selfless as possible (you'll find out otherwise in the next section). But my husband and I simply realized that we had enough—in fact, more than we needed—and there were so many who didn't.

Just for clarification, it's not as if every day since then our financial situation has been all rainbows and unicorns. We have had very real seasons of wondering how we were going to stay within our new boundaries, how we were going to make it work. We have had moments of temptation to cut our giving for a given month and get back on track the next month.

We have had many Jones family meetings in which we told our kids "no" to things that were important to them and explained why our family was making the choices we were. We have walked away from cushy job offers and taken significant pay cuts that have led us toward discomfort instead of away from it.

But to this day we have always been able to meet our family's needs, pay our bills and fulfill our monthly giving commitments. At times it has defied logic and simple math, yet God has always provided.

We have had random refund checks come in the mail, medical bills dissolved, anonymous gifts given—and the crazy part is, when our bank accounts have been the lowest, we have never felt more wealthy. Money cannot provide the kind of fulfillment that living in the fullness of Christ can provide.

Reason 2: We Want to Keep up With the Joneses

Oh, the irony of this idiom, my last name actually being Jones. As if having a name like Jenny and growing up during the Forrest Gump era (i.e., the 1960s) was not bad enough, I had to marry a guy with the last name Jones, creating the ultimate name combination of the late 1980s, early 1990s.

To this day, whenever I introduce myself, I hear one of three things: (1) "Jenaaaay, I love you, Jenaay"; (2) "Jenny Jones? Like that talk show host?"; or (3) "I guess we shouldn't try to keep up with those Joneses." (This last one typically happens when I am speaking about topics such as those covered in this book.) As my seven-year-old Seth would say, "That's a real knee-slapper!"

Sadly these days, an inability to keep up with our peers and their standards for success is perceived as socioeconomic failure.

I have never met someone who said aloud that his or her priority was to keep up with the Joneses—developing this outlook is far more of a gradual fade than that—but I *have* seen people convince themselves that their life is not good enough.

They talk themselves into throwing money away on things they would never have wanted if it wasn't for their friendly neighbors showing off their new purchases. This is such a psychological reality in the American mind that marketers have jumped on this concept in an effort to get people to buy their products. Volkswagen did an entire commercial completely centered on the fact that people will go to ridiculous lengths to keep up with the proverbial Joneses.[8]

In the midst of writing this book about excess, I fell into this trap—even if just for a moment. My husband and I typically split the responsibilities for dropping off our kids at school each morning. Chad takes the two older kids, and I take the two younger ones. But recently when my husband was out of town, I had to handle the tribe drop-off by myself.

On one particular day, my oldest daughter, Ryland, had choir practice and had to be at school forty minutes earlier than usual. As I sat in the carpool line at the elementary school, waiting for my turn to drop the kids off, Ryland was losing her cool because she was going to be late and therefore not be able to sing with her class at the retirement home later in the week.

I saw a dad drive his golf cart down the sidewalk—bypassing all of us stuck in the endless carpool line—right up to the school door, where his kids hopped out and headed into the school. It took him a total of three minutes to drop his kids off.

I immediately called my husband. "We need a golf cart!" I told him.

"What? Why? We don't even play golf or live on a golf course."

"Listen, if you are ever going out of town again, we need to buy a golf cart."

"Aren't you writing a book right now about excess?"

It's a good thing he wasn't in close proximity to me at that moment.

The Jones family (my actual family, not the mythical one in the idiom) is fortunate enough to be among the 9 percent of the world's population who owns a car;[9] despite that fact, for a brief moment I felt completely justified in our need for a golf cart. After all, it is super inconvenient to sit in my nice warm car with all of my children safely buckled into their age-appropriate car seats for ten minutes longer than I would have to if we had a golf cart. Then I came back to reality and thought, *For the love of everything good and holy, we don't even have a golf course in our neighborhood.*

Well, to prove how much God loves me and wants my book to be wildly successful, as I wrote this very sentence, I looked out the window of the coffee shop in which I was writing and saw a golf cart in the parking lot. I kid you not. (Y'all, I can't make this stuff up!)

There is not a golf course within ten miles of the coffee shop. And had I not seen that guy with his golf cart, the idea of needing a golf cart probably would never have entered my mind, because I can't recall ever feeling the need to own a golf cart before that moment. I can also guarantee you that in our previous neighborhood, where we had purchased our very first house, no one had owned a golf cart.

It's so interesting that as we move up the socioeconomic ladder, so do our financial commitments (e.g., mortgage payments, car loans, kids' extracurricular activities), and our need to keep up a certain image is not far behind. If we are not careful, we can find ourselves in a position where our finances cannot keep up with our desires.

This has to be one of the main contributing factors to the facts that the average credit card debt for indebted households in the United States stands at $15,355 (an increase of 1.95 percent over 2014), and the American consumer debt totals $11.91 trillion.[10] Keeping up with the Joneses is not the only reason for consumer debt; it is a much more complex issue than that. But the lure of comparison and of finding self-worth in the stuff we possess does drive us to make unwise purchases that we don't need and can't afford. This type of behavior keeps such financial gurus as Dave Ramsey, Suze Orman and Robert Kiyosaki selling books and scheduling speaking gigs.

Reason 3: We Are Isolated from Need

To be honest, this is the one that hit closest to home with me personally. When I went through my spiritual crisis two years ago and began to read the New Testament through, as I had promised to do, I was really struck by how the community of believers in Acts structured the entire church around taking care of each other and those in need.

As I began to pray through ways that I needed to implement what I was reading, one truth struck me with a healthy amount of embarrassment: I did not actually know one person in true physical need. Sure, I worked at a church and saw many people spiritually deprived, but real physical need—I could not have named a single individual.

This was not because poverty didn't exist in my community but, rather, it didn't exist in my social circle. I was isolated from hardship and did not intentionally seek ways to engage those in need. When I stopped and looked around my little world, I realized that everyone looked just like me, not only in appearance (that's another book) but also in standard of living. It is really hard to feel motivated to give when everyone around us seems to be doing just fine. On the other hand, it is really hard not to give when needs become more to us than just a sad TV commercial set to a Sarah McLachlan song[11]—when they become real people with names and faces trying desperately to provide for their families.

One night at Starbucks, I talked to a friend of mine about how I was beginning to feel a huge leading to engage with those in our community who had significant material needs, but I didn't want to come across as disrespectful or condescending. My friend invited me to go with her family on a Saturday morning to a church that distributed food, clothes and prayer to anyone who showed up.

That Saturday we headed to the Servant of Nations Church. As we approached the church, we saw a line of people that extended from the entrance of the church all the way down the street. The line included people of many different races and ages; there were mothers holding babies, as well as teenagers with their elderly grandparents.

I was assigned to clothes distribution, which I was incredibly thankful for, because on that particular Saturday it was pouring rain and super cold, and clothes distribution was inside the church while food distribution was outside.

I had brought Ryland with me, and I thought, *If we have to go outside at any point, I don't think we will be able to stay. I can't have her out in the wet and cold—she'll get sick.* Yet so many mothers were in the same dilemma. I had the choice of leaving and going to a grocery store to get food for my family—but maybe these mamas didn't. Maybe their choice was between feeding their little ones that week or risking their kids getting sick. My daughter and I worked with a group of other volunteers the entire morning organizing, hanging up, and distributing clothes. I remember so clearly the pivotal moment of the morning for me.

After everyone waiting in line had gone through the clothes and food stations, a volunteer looked at me and said, "Would you like me to pick up a box of food for your family?" She probably thought for a brief second that I was either deaf or crazy, because I stared at her blankly. My mind was having a hard time comprehending her question. Of course I didn't need a box of food—I was here to help give stuff away, not to take it for myself.

Finally, I snapped out of it and said, "No, we are fine." She replied back, "Are you sure? One of the pastors here always holds a few boxes back, so we can serve and still get food for ourselves." All I could do was muster up another, "No. I'm good."

In that moment I realized how isolated I was from those in need and that I had a very skewed perception of poverty and those affected by it.[12] In my mind everyone fit neatly into his or her own place in society. People either gave to those who needed help or took what someone else offered them. No one did both.

I'm so incredibly ashamed to say that deep down I believed that poverty only existed for those who were drug addicts or jobless and who didn't do anything about their need. I believed that poverty was a clear-cut issue and that those in poverty weren't trying hard enough, weren't taking advantage of education, weren't making wise decisions or weren't willing to take whatever job was available.

Of course, some people take advantage of the system, but to make that sweeping claim about everyone in poverty is simply narrow-minded. But even when people take advantage of the system, does it really matter as far as the gospel is concerned? Did Jesus not die for those people as well?

That day I made friends with people whose socioeconomic status was much lower than mine. I had no knowledge of this until our friendships were already made. That day I realized that poverty is complex; and while various solutions are needed to make an impact on this societal issue, judgment and ignorance are not part of the solution. That day poverty had a face, a name and a story—none of which lined up with my preconceived notions.

Reason 4: Leaping Is Not Secure

When was the last time you really needed God to show up? The last time you were desperate to see Him move? Most of our answers to that question normally have to do with situations outside our control in which we have no choice but to depend on God, because there is simply nothing we can do to change the circumstances.

Illness is a good example of this. Unfortunately, I had the experience of walking through cancer with my mom a couple of years ago. It was a turbulent ride for our family, and eventually we had to come to the place where we accepted that we could not control the situation.

We could not make the medicine work, we could not become oncologists overnight and oversee my mom's treatment, and we could not walk this road for her. But even if we could have done all these things, we still could not have guaranteed her healing or the preservation of her life.

Cancer stinks; and if you ask my mom, she could give her own account of why this is true and what she learned from being sick. As for me, I learned the freedom that comes from being in a situation that I was completely unable to control.

Up until that point in my life, I had never been in a situation in which I really needed God to come through. But I also had never been in a situation in which I experienced what it looked like when He didn't (at least, when He didn't in the way I thought He should).

Sure, I had prayed and had things not go my way (and I had thrown little toddler fits about it), but I'd never faced problems of real importance. Cancer taught me that not being in control is scary and insecure, but it never changes who God is; that not being in control causes me to feel incredibly chaotic, but there is still a rock-solid peace that God is who He says He is. Even if I could not physically see God, I could choose to believe Him in my heart. Even in my uncertainty I knew that He was secure.

Walking through my mom's cancer with her was a real-life illustration to me of faith. I had thought I knew what faith was; but until faith is our only option, we don't really know what it is—not as it is defined in Hebrews 11:1, anyway: "Faith is confidence in what we hope for and assurance about what we do not see."

The ironic thing is that I walked away from that experience not jaded, angry or bitter but, rather, wondering why I hadn't pursued complete and unadulterated surrender before. I found myself wishing that I had been intentional about putting myself in positions of faith instead of having to be forced there.

But taking a leap of faith is not secure; staying on the ground is secure. Leaping is scary. There was a pure exhilaration in completely trusting the Lord and watching Him work in ways that I would never have imagined or experienced had I not leaped.

For one week every year, the staff at the church where I worked for nine years went to a thousand-acre hunting ranch in the hill country of the greatest state ever to exist—Texas (yes, I am one of those Texans).

While on staff retreat a few years ago, we made a video to illustrate the leap that faith requires. We blindfolded our student pastor Chris and sent him walking across a field that appeared to end abruptly with a nasty cliff. We filmed Chris as he walked, came to the end of the field and then walked off the side of the mountain. At least that's what we intended our film's viewers to think. What they would not be able to see was the ledge on the other side of the cliff showing that Chris had been perfectly safe the whole time.

Committing to engage with, give to and help those in need will many times lead us to the edge of a cliff. We will find ourselves looking over the edge and having to decide whether to turn around and follow the path back to what we know is secure or leap off the edge into the unknown. We can't see the ledge on the other side of the cliff—but God can.

Our staff members weren't stressed about Chris getting hurt or falling to his death. In fact, at one point we had to reshoot because he tripped over some barbwire, and we laughed hysterically at his seeming demise. We say "no" to so many things that the Lord is asking of us (big things, little things, important things, stupid things) because we think that leaping is not secure. Yet the whole time God is saying, "I see the other side; it's safe. I got this."

This is what Chad and I discovered when we stepped into the true blessing of not living the safe, secure and, honestly, generally faithless life. Once we experienced God's powerful provision, there was no turning back, and Christianity wasn't so boring for us anymore.

Untangling Ourselves

Ten years before my spiritual crisis, during the summer between my freshman and sophomore years in college, I did a twelve-week internship for the Southern Baptist Convention's International Mission Board in India. There I was exposed to genuine physical need.

I got to visit a Mother Teresa Home, and I looked into the faces of dying people who had been shunned by family, friends and society. I saw children in their last days of starvation; and I saw women and girls being exploited, sexually abused and forced into marriage with men decades older than them.

I also experienced families inviting me into their homes and cooking what I am confident was their entire food supply for that week to make sure I felt welcomed by their hospitality. I witnessed a grown man listening intently to a college-aged American girl fumbling through sharing the gospel in a culture in which women do not openly speak about spiritual matters to men. I watched his entire family decide to follow Jesus for the rest of their lives.

As I traveled back to the United States, I thought and prayed, *I will never be the same after this. Do other people know what is happening in other parts of the world? We have to fix this.* In that moment I meant every word. Yet just ten short years later, I was living in the suburbs, wondering how in the world Chad and I were going to manage three kids without a third row in our SUV. Hello!

The tricky thing about pursuing the American dream is that we don't embrace it in a dramatic transformation; it creeps up on us slowly and then ensnares us tightly. When we realize that we have been trapped, we struggle to find a way out.

As I explained the premise of this chapter to my husband, he said to me, "Okay, so how are normal people supposed to address this problem of being caught up in the American dream?"

"Normal people? What do you mean?"

"Yeah, normal people," he said. "Not people like you—pastor people or people who do everything with dramatic sweeping gestures. I'm talking about people who don't have extremist, go-big-or-go-home personality types like you do. You know, normal people."

I stared daggers of death at him.

As much as I hated to admit it, he was right. Not everyone will feel called to haul off and sell a house, adopt a kid or commit to give away half their income. But how different would our world look if everyone did? Still, I get it. We all have dinner to prepare, laundry to do, kids to get ready for bed, dishes to put away and hopes of getting some sleep. When and how are we supposed to find time to take on the world? If we can boil it down to a starting point, it simply starts with redefining our definition of "blessing."

3

Blessed Are the Empty

When I began reading the New Testament after my spiritual crisis, I wanted to get the most authentic picture of Jesus possible. I needed a compass of truth to compare everything in my life to, because I was struggling to see a life or culture around me that resembled that of the New Testament, and I felt my hope diminishing. I also made the commitment to read everything Jesus said as if He meant it *literally*. This is tricky, especially in John 6 where Jesus starts talking about eating flesh and drinking blood.

> Jesus said to them, "Very truly I tell you, unless you eat the flesh of the Son of Man and drink his blood, you have no life in you. Whoever eats my flesh and drinks my blood has eternal life, and I will raise them up at the last day. For my flesh is real food and my blood is real drink. Whoever eats my flesh and drinks my blood remains in me, and I in them. Just as the living Father sent me and I live because of the Father, so the one who feeds on me will live because of me. (6:53–57)

At my former church, every Thursday morning our pastor did a little exercise called "sermon run through." He preached his entire Sunday sermon just for our staff, and we told him what we liked or thought could be improved. All I'm saying is that on that particular day Jesus' disciples may have wished they'd had a run through.

Now before my poor publisher gets inundated with e-mails and hate letters about how I am trying to say that Jesus needed to be corrected, I'm not. I'm just saying that there was no way His disciples were prepared for that, and they probably weren't convinced that it was the best strategy for growth. They were probably thinking, *Jesus, don't You understand that people already think You're crazy? This is not helping!* But Jesus is perfect, and we are not.

But back to my Bible reading. It didn't take me long, only five chapters into the New Testament, before I got to the Beatitudes (see Matt. 5:3–12). I became borderline obsessed with this passage, because it gave some real insight into how the American dream has completely distorted our view of what a blessed life should look like.

The name "Beatitudes" is derived from the Latin word *beatus*, which means "blessed," and each verse in this passage starts off with the phrase "Blessed are." That little phrase "blessed are" is what captivated me and totally blew up the American dream for me. As I read these ten verses over and over again, I realized that I had been misinterpreting what a blessed life was; in fact, I had been misinterpreting the very definition of the word "blessed" my entire life. And I don't think I'm the only one in that boat. I would even go out on a limb and say that churches in the Western world in general have completely redefined what a blessed life should look like. And its definition does not line up with what Jesus says in these ten verses. Rather, at times, it is in stark contrast to His teaching.

To fully understand the weight of these verses, we have to understand the context in which Matthew places them in his Gospel. The Beatitudes are the introduction to what later became known as the Sermon on the Mount (see Matt. 5–7), which is by far Jesus' most well-known sermon. Many people believe that the Sermon on the Mount was preached late in Jesus' ministry but that Matthew may have put it in the early part of his book in order to state up front the characteristics of a life that reflects the kingdom of God.

Dr. Allen Ross, formerly professor of New Testament and Hebrew at Beeson Divinity School, says it like this: "These qualities give a picture of the character of the true people of God, those who are a part of his kingdom and have the full blessings of the kingdom to look forward to. Taken together they give the picture of the perfect disciple of Christ who is the heir of the promises."[1] Pretty staunch words—"the picture of the perfect disciple of Christ."

The Beatitudes also come after Jesus made a call to repentance (see 4:17), indicating that the first thing that must happen before any form of discipleship can take place is repentance—our initial salvation. Following that, the characteristics reflecting a kingdom-minded life cannot develop until *full* repentance has taken place—the complete surrendering of our rights and wills to God for whatever He wants to do with us. Otherwise, we are back at just checking a list.

The other thing to note about the Beatitudes is that while, yes, they are part of the larger narrative of the Sermon on the

Mount, we cannot read the Beatitudes like any other narrative or parable.

The Beatitudes are like proverbs, each one with its own topic and agenda, and each one should be studied individually. That's why we are going to look at the first three in this chapter and tackle the other six in the next two chapters.

The Beatitudes use words or phrases that we don't hear much today but were commonly used in Jewish culture in Jesus' day—words and phrases such as "poor in spirit," "meek," "pure in heart" and "peacemaker."

We will address these as we come to them in the text, but the first word we need to clearly define—the word that creates the basic premise for this entire book—is the word "blessed."

These days we align the word "blessed" with fulfillment or even happiness that is attached to things like houses, cars, retirement accounts, clothes, vacations and even immaterial things like health, family and careers.

But in the Beatitudes the word "blessed" describes the inner joy and peace that come from following Christ and aligning our character with the heart of God.

Not surprisingly, many of us have so distorted the true meaning of blessing. Something as intangible as inner joy is incredibly difficult to measure or describe. Instagramming inner peace is also really hard. We find it much easier to work hard every day, make money, buy something we want and call that blessing.

So let's take a look at each beatitude individually. We will look at the meaning of some of the key words in each one and then talk about its application to our lives. Let's go!

Blessed Are the Poor in Spirit

Have you ever heard someone say that Christianity is a crutch for those who aren't strong enough to make it on their own? This common idea has been stated in many different ways and is typically used as a way to disprove Christianity or the reality of God. But the idea of Christianity being a crutch is the foundation of the first beatitude: "Blessed are the poor in spirit, for theirs is the kingdom of heaven" (Matt. 5:3).

Being poor in spirit is realizing that we cannot do things all on our own and that we need a support system. It's knowing that God is all-powerful and that we are not, that we cannot save ourselves, that we are dying and desperately need a Savior.

Being poor in spirit is recognizing that God is our real source of happiness and fulfillment. This means that whether we have more than we need or not enough, we are equally blessed, because being poor in spirit is a conscious decision to humble ourselves before the Lord. It is a mind-set, not a standard of living.

This is why people who, from a worldly perspective, are impoverished can also be filled with a contagious joy—such people are poor in spirit. The same is true the other way as well—people who, from a worldly perspective, have it all can be terribly miserable.

When I was in India, I was given the project of hand drawing a map for the city of Varanasi. The International Mission Board was about to send a family of missionaries to live in Varanasi, but they did not have an updated map (or really any map at all) to give the family to help them get around town.

Now, I am not artistically talented—like at all. In junior high school I was required to take at least one semester of art, and I was so truly terrible that I actually had to go to after-school tutoring for a class that 99 percent of eighth graders consider a cakewalk. So as you can imagine, cartography was not right up my alley.

Upon arriving in Varanasi, I began planning how I would tackle this project. Because I would be there for eight weeks, I mentally split the city into eight sections and planned to tackle one section a week. However, I would never be able to finish in the eight-week time frame if I had to walk the entire city, so I immediately began a search for a driver. My funds were limited, and I did not know the language well enough to maneuver the public transportation system, so I eventually settled on the driver of an auto rickshaw.

Auto rickshaw used for transportation in India

My driver's name was Manish. He had been born and raised in Varanasi, he was married and had two children, and he spoke very broken English. But broken English was better than no English. I could not afford to hire him at his hourly rate for eight weeks, so he made a deal with me for $20 a day (more than he would normally make) and English lessons. Manish was a living illustration to me of being poor in spirit. On so many days when I walked to the parking lot from my hotel room, I was in no way in a positive state of mind. I was homesick, it was blazing hot (like 112 degrees Fahrenheit), everything was dirty and I had no idea how to draw a stinkin' map. Yet Manish greeted me each morning with a huge smile, asked me what adventure we were going on today and happily served me for the whole day.

This was a man who made roughly $6,000 a year, worked outside in temperatures that I can only describe as hellacious and went home to a one-room house with dirt floors and no running water or electricity.

I know this to be true, because remember that college-aged girl who stumbled through the gospel but whom God used anyway to lead a family to Christ? Yeah, the college-aged girl was me, and the family was Manish's.

Most people would agree that Manish would have been more than justified in being bitter about his circumstances, yet he was not. Just being around him was a blessing, and his passion for his job and his city was contagious. He was truly poor in spirit.

Together he and I finished that map—he proudly showing me around his city and I drawing it. During my last week in India, Manish invited me to his house for dinner, and I had the best time sitting on the floor eating with his family and laughing until we cried about all the stupid American things I had done over the last eight weeks. I went home that night hoping that my family would one day be as blessed as Manish's family.

What blessing do we gain from being poor in spirit? Well, Jesus said that we will gain the kingdom of heaven, which in Manish's case was absolutely true. However, the opposite is also true—if we are not poor in spirit, we won't gain the kingdom of heaven. Essentially, Jesus was saying right off the bat that to gain the kingdom of heaven, we must empty ourselves of dependence on ourselves or the thinking that we deserve anything.

Becoming poor in spirit is a two-part process: (1) recognizing our sinful nature and the divide that our sin puts between us and God, and (2) accepting the forgiveness offered us through Jesus' death on the cross.

But being poor in spirit does not stop there. It is not just for those who don't know the gospel; it is also a continual process of discipleship for those who follow Christ. Being poor in spirit is not something we achieve one time and then check off our list; it is something that we have to intentionally pursue on an ongoing basis.

Blessed Are Those Who Mourn

The first beatitude about becoming poor in spirit is followed by the second beatitude: "Blessed are those who mourn, for they will be comforted" (Matt. 5:4). Once we pursue being poor in spirit, a deep sense of mourning over the gravity of our sin and how it separates us from community with God will follow.

When we think of mourning, we often think of something that has been lost, whether a loved one, an opportunity or something that should have been. But in Matthew 5:4 mourning has to do with our individual sinful condition, as well as the sinful condition of others.

I am smack dab in the middle of this beatitude right now as I deeply mourn the condition of our world. An example of this is the violent terrorist attacks that took place on November 13, 2015, in Paris, France at six different locations virtually simultaneously, one at a soccer stadium and another at a concert hall.

These were not battlefields or places of destruction, but places where people had gone to create joy-filled memories. The death toll was 130, and 368 were injured. The country of Syria had been taken over by members of the same terrorist group that perpetrated the Paris attacks, and many Syrians are fighting back or fleeing from the evil that lurks at their doorstep.

Several countries, however, have denied entrance to Syrian refugees, many of whom are dying in the process of trying to provide safety for their families. In the days following the attacks in Paris, the governors of twenty-eight US states said they would refuse Syrian refugees sent to their states. One of them was the governor of Texas, the state I call home.

I watched on social media as many of my Christian friends picked sides and openly mocked, criticized and berated each other in opposition. I found myself typing and then deleting my own statuses charged by anger and disappointment.

I questioned and judged people's ability to call themselves Christians, until I finally realized that I was more caught up in the response to the refugee crisis than I was in actually doing something to aid the refugees. I deeply mourned the root of sin in my own reaction, along with the hate-filled, evil acts of the terrorists. The paralyzing sense of hopelessness I felt angered me, and it seemed as if I could do nothing except hide in fear or respond in ignorance.

But then I remembered the promise of this beatitude—the promise that those who mourn will be comforted. Jesus' point in this beatitude is that if our mourning is rooted in the fact that we are broken people living in a broken world, He will be quick to comfort us with the vision of an eternal kingdom that is not of this world.

What are we mourning? Better yet, what do we need to mourn? We can't start filling up our lives with the real blessing God has for us until we empty it of the sinful attitudes that are not of Him and allow Him complete control in our lives and in the circumstances around us.

Jesus was keenly aware of the process needed to become truly blessed; that is why He started the Beatitudes with a call to repentance, or to being poor in spirit, which will lead us to a true sense of mourning over of the weight of our sin and the sin around us.

Blessed Are the Meek

In the third beatitude we find one of those words that no one ever uses—like ever. Not only can I not name one time when I have used the word "meek" (outside of writing this book, of course), I don't know that I have ever heard someone else use this word except when talking about this verse. But Jesus said, "Blessed are the meek, for they will inherit the earth" (Matt. 5:5).

Maybe we never hear this word because meekness has developed such a negative, weak connotation in our society. We are taught that if we are meek, people will take advantage of us and walk all over us.

In fact, if we look up the word "meek" in the dictionary, we find definitions like "overly submissive," "compliant," "spiritless" and "tame." However, the dictionary also tells us that an obsolete definition of meek (one that is no longer used) is "gentle" and "kind."[2] This definition is more in line with what Jesus was saying. In reality, people who are meek will never take advantage of someone; rather, they are the first to defend those being taken advantage of or exploited. (I think our society could benefit from a few more leaders in our midst who fit this "obsolete" definition.)

In this biblical context, meekness means handing over our cause to God and trusting Him with it to the point that we don't have to defend ourselves. But doesn't that go against everything in us? We are taught from a young age to fight for things, to stand up for ourselves. If something is worth committing to, then we are taught to do everything we can to defend it.

But Jesus' command to be meek is quite the opposite perspective. He knows the desires of our hearts; He knows our needs; He knows our dreams. And He has already begun a work in each of us that will not go unfinished.

We don't need to manipulate events, deceive anyone, or help God out! We don't need to fear loss because those who are meek will inherit the earth! We can take big leaps of faith and trust that God will take care of our dreams and our needs!

I know how obnoxiously positive this must sound. Being meek is so much easier said than done. To give our desires over to God and not pick them up again, even when things aren't happening quite fast enough, is incredibly hard. An insurmountable amount of self-control is required.

But here is the irony: that dream, that desire, that thing that we can't release—who do we think created it in us? It was God. And He would not have put it there if He did not intend for us to see fruition. Meekness is not confining or haltering—it's actually freeing. It frees us from the pressure of bearing the weight of responsibility and allows us to simply sit back and enjoy the ride.

John Piper defines meekness beautifully.

> Meekness begins when we put our trust in God. Then, because we trust Him, we commit our way to Him. We

> roll onto Him our anxieties, our frustrations, our plans, our relationships, our jobs, our health. And then we wait patiently for the Lord. We trust His timing and His power and His grace to work things out in the best way for His glory and for our good.
>
> The result of trusting God and the rolling of our anxieties onto God and waiting patiently for God is that we don't give way to quick and fretful anger. But instead, like Moses we give place to wrath and hand our cause over to God and let him vindicate us if He chooses. And then, as James says, in this quiet confidence we are slow to speak and quick to listen. We become reasonable and open to correction. Meekness loves to learn. And it counts the blows of a friend as precious. And when it must say a critical word to a person caught in sin or error, it speaks from the deep conviction of its own fallibility and its own susceptibility to sin and its utter dependence on the grace of God.[3]

Unfortunately, we don't meet truly meek people very often; but when we do, we know it. They are magnetic. They make a lasting impression that is hard to shake, and we can't help but want to be around them.

Meekness is a genuine authenticity that is hard to find in our media-driven world. Meekness is striking in a world in which people can make their lives look any way they desire through pictures, hashtags and a few phrases.

I have had the wonderful privilege of meeting several people whom I would not hesitate to describe as meek. Rob Morris is the cofounder and president of Love146, an international human rights organization working to end child sex trafficking and exploitation—truly the most horrific injustice that exists in our world right now—through survivor care and prevention education.[4]

United Nations International Children's Emergency Fund (UNICEF) explains child trafficking this way:

> Child victims of trafficking are recruited, transported, transferred, harbored or received for the purpose of exploitation. They may be forced to work in sweatshops, on construction sites or in houses as domestic servants; on the streets as child beggars, in wars as child soldiers, on farms, in traveling sales crews or in restaurants and hotels. Some are forced to work in brothels and strip clubs or for escort and massage services.[5]

I have had many conversations with Rob and found something so captivating about him, and after studying this beatitude I realized that it was meekness. Rob is the very definition of a person who has an insurmountable amount of self-control and a belief in God's love conquering every inch of darkness and evil that exist in the horrific child-trafficking industry. His meekness is seen in the story of how Love146 was founded.

> We found ourselves standing shoulder to shoulder with predators in a small room, looking at young girls through a pane of glass. All of the girls wore red dresses with a number pinned to their dress for identification.
>
> They sat, blankly watching cartoons on TV. They were vacant, shells of what a child should be. There was no light in their eyes, no life left. Their light had been taken from them. These children . . . raped each night . . . seven, ten, fifteen times every night. They were so young. Thirteen,

> eleven . . . it was hard to tell. Sorrow covered their faces with nothingness.
>
> Except one girl. One girl who wouldn't watch the cartoons. Her number was 146. She was looking beyond the glass. She was staring out at us with a piercing gaze. There was still fight left in her eyes. There was still life left in this girl. . . .
>
> All of these emotions begin to wreck you. Break you. It is agony. It is aching. It is grief. It is sorrow.
>
> The reaction is intuitive, instinctive. It is visceral. It releases a wailing cry inside of you. It elicits gut-level indignation. It is unbearable. I remember wanting to break through the glass. To take her away from that place. To scoop up as many of them as I could into my arms. To take all of them away. I wanted to break through the glass to tell her to keep fighting. To not give up. To tell her that we were coming for her. . . .
>
> Because we went in as part of an ongoing undercover investigation on this particular brothel, we were unable to immediately respond. Evidence had to be collected in order to bring about a raid—and, eventually, justice—on those running the brothel. It is an immensely difficult problem when an immediate response cannot address an emergency. Some time later, there was a raid on this brothel, but the children we saw, including the girl who wore #146, were no longer there. We do not know what happened to her, but we will never forget her. She changed the course of all of our lives.[6]

Rob says that participating in that undercover mission, and making a commitment to not compromise it in any way, was the hardest thing he has ever done in his entire life, and it went against everything inside him.

The only thing that allowed him to keep his composure was the larger vision of developing a strategy that would work to completely shut down this industry, and that is exactly what he has pursued. Trusting this beautiful child into God's hands when there was nothing Rob could do to change her situation is a perfect picture of meekness.

Rob passionately advocates for children who desperately need to be rescued; but in the same conversation he will bring to light the fact that many of the people running these industries were themselves exploited and abused as children, and they too need love and forgiveness. I mean, who does that? Someone who is meek, that's who.

I have never once heard Rob be territorial or judgmental of other organizations also fighting against child trafficking, even those that use a different strategy than Love146. He never claims to have all the answers on how to end the trafficking problem; he is just thankful that there are fighters in the game. He does not earn the salary that most CEOs of international nonprofits earn, because he believes in using as much of the donated funds as possible to help children. And this is a concept that runs throughout the entire organization.

I have never seen Rob get angry about an ignorant question regarding trafficking; he patiently answers and finds hope in the fact that at least people are talking about it. Even when I have been fired up in conversation with Rob and have not shown much meekness toward individuals or organizations that, in my opinion, are clumsy in communicating the stories of victims, Rob has not one time joined in. Instead, he has responded a lot like Jesus, having faith that in the end God will win, justice will prevail and evil will be overtaken.

I never pass up an opportunity to spend time with Rob, because his passion moves people to action—not because he is pushy, but because he is meek. When we put our cause in God's hands and leave it with Him, we are blessed indeed.

Emptying Ourselves

As we wrap up these first three beatitudes, note the common theme that runs through them: personal emptiness. Each one focuses on intentionally emptying ourselves in order that we may be filled by God.

We empty ourselves of a false self-reliance that keeps us bound in the chains of sin and become poor in spirit; then we empty ourselves of our sin and mourn over our brokenness and the brokenness of the world around; and, finally, we empty ourselves of pride and intentionally seek humility and meekness. Jesus knew that God is jealous and holy and will not—no, better yet, cannot—coexist with our self-reliance, sin and pride. According to Jesus, a blessed life is one that reflects continual dependence on Him, recognition and repentance of sin, and a heart of surrendered humility.

But the Beatitudes don't end there. Jesus started with the theme of emptiness because He knew that emptiness is always followed by a hunger and thirst for something that will fill us once again.

Blessed are the empty.

4

For They Will Be Filled

We all have an inherent restlessness in us—a desire to be a part of something larger than ourselves and to do something significant with our lives. The problem is, many of us try to accomplish this through materialism, addictions, earthly relationships or even the achievements of religion, but these things simply cannot satiate this stirring inside us.

This is why my checklist for God was not able to erase the discontent I felt inside. Actually, I don't think it's possible for us to erase our discontent.

We are purposefully designed with a spirit of dissatisfaction with lesser things, because it is the driving force behind a progressing relationship with Christ. It is a gentle reminder that we were not created for a happy life of self-fulfillment but, rather, for glorifying God through building His kingdom and loving people. That is exactly what these next three beatitudes are about.

When a genuine Christ follower empties himself of worldly pleasure and pursuits and becomes ready to depend on a big

God, he is then in the extraordinary position to be able to be filled by God. This is a perfect picture of a truly blessed life.

Blessed Are Those Who Hunger and Thirst for Righteousness

Two of the most basic human needs are food and water, and Jesus uses these needs as imagery in the next beatitude: "Blessed are those who hunger and thirst for righteousness, for they will be filled" (Matt. 5:6). These two needs are powerful—so powerful, in fact, that starvation has been used as a torture tactic during times of war or interrogation.

When a person is truly hungry or dehydrated, that individual can't think straight (some even have intense hallucinations), and having the need for food or water met is the only thing consuming the person's mind. An underfed body emits pain until it is nourished.

School districts offer free or reduced-price lunches, because teachers and administrators know that children with hungry bellies will not have the capacity to learn in their classrooms. Basic needs must be met before further growth can take place.

Hunger and thirst are used as analogies in this beatitude, because everyone can relate to and fully understand this concept. It is an understandable barometer of the level at which we should desire righteousness in our lives. Righteousness is not simply a certain level of morality that we should hope to achieve; rather, it is a need so strong that it must be satisfied.

The concept of righteousness in Matthew 5:6 refers to a hunger and thirst for personal righteousness, but it also indicates that we should desire righteousness for the rest of the world. The two cannot be separated, and the quest for one should overflow to the other.

Hungering and Thirsting for Personal Righteousness

To really hunger and thirst for personal righteousness, we have to want to be purified. We have to understand what our sin does to our relationship with God. Just like any other relationship in our lives, when someone hurts us with their words or actions, it creates a roadblock in our ability to connect with them.

Any time my husband and I have unresolved conflict, it quickly infiltrates our ability to communicate with each other, show affection or stay on the same page regarding our family. The longer we go without addressing that conflict, the harder it becomes to reconnect. We become more like ships passing in the night than partners.

Sin does the same thing to our relationship with God; it prevents us from experiencing fellowship with Him. We stop hearing His voice clearly—or at all. We begin to develop our own agendas. Some shiny new thing distracts us, and gradually we and the Lord become like passing ships in the night. Sin keeps us from aligning our lives with the Bible, and instead we begin to align our lives with other things that are important to us. As long as we don't become truly bad people, we think we are okay.

Our standard of righteousness is set by comparison to others instead of by God's Word. How many times have we said to ourselves, "Well, sure, I could do better. I mean, I'm not perfect, but I'm doing better than so-and-so!"

But here's the thing—that doesn't matter! God has called each of us to a specific purpose, and it is only based on bringing Him glory. It has nothing to do with anyone else. Our hunger and thirst for righteousness cannot be based on a standard set by anyone except the Lord. We also have to acknowledge that only God can fill us. Could it be that we can never get our desires for something more—an adventure, a life filled with purpose and significance, a mission—satiated because we are trying to fill our lives with the pursuit of temporal things rather than the central pursuit of righteousness?

When I think back two years ago to the night of my spiritual crisis, when I looked at Chad in complete desperation, I now know that I was so thirsty for the righteousness of God and so empty from the shallowness of what this world has to offer that I needed to be filled.

The process of hungering for righteousness is simply sanctification, which means to be "set apart" for a purpose. God has set *you and me* apart for a purpose; we must never allow a temporary thrill to get in the way of the lifelong adventure that God has already marked out for us.

If we wonder what areas of our lives need to go through the refining process of sanctification, here is a surefire way to figure it out: We can say, "I really hope God doesn't ask me to give up ____________." When we get to the point at which we can change that statement to "God, being in Your will is more important to me than anything that You could ever ask me to give up, so before You even ask the question, I say 'yes,'" then we are hungry for God's righteousness.

Desiring Righteousness for the Rest of the World

Pursuing personal righteousness does not equal isolation from the world. It also does not mean judgment on the rest of the world. I absolutely love this quote from Andy Stanley: "Everybody matters to God, whether or not God matters to them."[1]

Remember, one of the keys to a blessed life is meekness—God does not need us to protect Him or stick up for Him when we see darkness in the world around us; He needs us to show love to the world.

Desiring righteousness for the rest of the world is not putting up a snarky social media post and hoping that everyone on the other side of the political spectrum reads it and is magically transformed into someone just like us . . . I mean, the person God created them to be. It's not expressed through condemnation but, rather, through empathy and love.

When we begin to desire righteousness for the world, it is an overflow of our pursuit of personal righteousness. It comes from having personally journeyed from brokenness to restoration and then wanting that healing for the rest of the world. When was the last time you really prayed for our world, and not in the Southern "Oh bless your heart, I'll pray for you" kind of way? I'm talking the on-your-knees, crying-out-to-God kind of way.

One thing that helps us do this is to couple the spiritual discipline of prayer with fasting. Eugene H. Merrill, professor emeritus of Old Testament studies at Dallas Theological Seminary, describes fasting like this:

> The purpose of fasting is never explicitly stated in Scripture but its connection to penitence, mourning and supplication suggests a self-denial that opens one to God and to the immaterial aspects of life. Inasmuch as food and drink typify life in the flesh and all its demands and satisfactions, their absence or rejection speaks to the reality of a higher dimension, one in which the things of the spirit predominate. The theology of fasting, then, is a theology of priorities in which believers are given the opportunity to express themselves in an undivided and intensive devotion to the Lord and to the concerns of the spiritual life.[2]

I don't fast because I'm some sort of spiritual giant in the ranks of Moses or Paul. Most of the time I fast because I have a sin in my life that is becoming a stronghold or because someone I deeply care for needs intercession as they also walk the road to freedom. Fasting gives me a hunger for God's righteousness—literally.

One time Pastor Mike, the minister at the church where I worked, asked the staff to join him in fasting for God to move in the lives of the families in our community.

He asked us to first spend a week or so praying and asking God how He wanted us to fast, as there are many different ways,[3] and then to meet back and share with each other what we were going to do, so we could encourage each other.

That week I prayed to the Lord about how He wanted me to participate in our corporate fast, and He impressed on my heart that I was to support my pastor by fasting in whatever way he felt the Lord was leading him. When the staff gathered around our conference room table, I purposefully sat next to our pastor so that, as each of us took a turn telling the others how we were going to fast, I could speak after him.

When it was Mike's turn, he said, "I feel that the Lord wants to move in a powerful way in our community, and we need to be serious about asking Him to do that. I want to be more dependent on Him than ever before, so I am going to do fourteen days of water only."

"Well, crap!" I said.

"Excuse me?" Mike said, looking at me.

"I also will be doing fourteen days, water only."

The next fourteen days were the most physically taxing of my life. I was exhausted constantly. From day eleven on I had to decide every morning between showering and dressing up—if

I showered, I simply put on workout clothes to wear to work; and if I didn't shower, I was able to put on work clothes and makeup. I simply did not have the energy to both shower and fix myself up.

But in that time I cried out to the Lord on behalf of my city and community as I never had before. I begged the Lord to break the addictions of materialism, discontent and selfishness that I saw throughout our community. I prayed that we would develop a reputation of having ridiculous amounts of generosity—and not just for our well-to-do, master-planned communities.

I prayed that God would move on the hearts of families to become foster parents and that no child in our county would have to spend another day without a family. I prayed that my beloved city of Houston would no longer carry the title of the largest child sex-trafficking hub in the United States but, rather, would be instrumental in ending child sex trafficking across the world.

I prayed that the power and truth of the gospel of Jesus Christ would penetrate the lives and hearts of the people in my neighborhood and city. I desired deeply to see righteousness in my community; I literally and figuratively hungered and thirsted for it.

Although my prayers were fervent and pure, here's the irony: I was not actively seeking any of those things in my own life. My family did give 10 percent to our church (mostly because I was on staff and, well, it just didn't seem right to take money from the church but not give any)—not what I would qualify as ridiculous generosity. We weren't actively involved in the process of fostering or adopting, nor did we even know someone we could support in that process.

We had written a check once to Love146 to help fight child trafficking, but we knew that God had been asking us to do more. We simply had never found the time to get involved (as if anything we were doing was as important as fighting child trafficking!). And, as I mentioned before, I didn't personally know anyone I would qualify as living in real poverty.

What started out as a fast for my community quickly led to some real conviction and purifying in my own life, because, remember, our desire to see righteousness in the rest of the world has to come from an overflow of hungering for righteousness in our own lives.

Being righteous is not synonymous with being perfect. It simply means that we have enough humility to realize that we are flawed, broken people in need of God's righteousness in order to live out His purpose for our lives. That kind of pursuit leads right into the next two beatitudes: being merciful and pure in heart.

Blessed Are the Merciful

For years, when I read Matthew 5:7, "Blessed are the merciful, for they will be shown mercy," I thought it meant that I needed to show mercy to people when they messed up because I would need mercy shown to me when I messed up. Sort of an "I'll scratch your back, and you scratch mine" or "what goes around comes around" mind-set. That motivation is so messed up and not at all what Jesus means in this verse, mainly because if mercy could be earned, like a wage, then it would no longer be mercy. Extending mercy means not giving someone the punishment he or she deserves. This is exactly what Paul was trying to get across to the Ephesians when he said, "Be kind and compassionate to one another, forgiving each other, just as in Christ God forgave you" (Eph. 4:32).

We need to freely offer mercy to others, because it represents the mercy that God freely offers to us on a daily basis. But extending mercy is difficult for a lot of the same reasons that being meek is difficult. We have been raised to believe that people's actions produce consequences, sometimes positive and sometimes negative, and they are responsible for their own choices.

If someone is suffering consequences from his own bad decision, then he made his bed—let him lie in it, right? Though this might be true, what it doesn't take into account is our ability as Christ followers to *choose* to extend mercy instead of judgment, just as Christ did for us.

I often see this unmerciful attitude in many Christians toward the homeless community, which is interesting, because no one sets out with a goal to be homeless. People find themselves homeless for a variety of reasons,[4] and it is rarely because of laziness. Yet I often hear comments like, "They just need to get a job" or "They could have a different life if they really wanted to."

This is where that pesky American dream comes into play. We are perfectly comfortable helping the homeless in other countries, but it's different in America—here there is no excuse for being homeless. We want to believe that America is better at equal opportunity than it really is.

But it is incredibly difficult to "just get a job" for a person who has no contact information to put on forms or a resume, no access to clean, professional-looking clothes for an interview and no place to shower. And let's just assume someone can get over all those obstacles—even then, convincing a manager to hire him or her with an unsteady living situation is nearly impossible.

I don't know the last time you tried to live on the street (if you were able to buy this book, I'm going to venture out and say never); but from my observations, it is exhausting and not an environment in which a lazy person could survive.

Many homeless people are sleep-deprived, sick (both physically and mentally) and victims of broken family relationships. While they can apply for assistance—when their biggest worries are finding safety, food and shelter—they are often in no condition to maneuver the bureaucracy of government assistance.

Taking care of the homeless and impoverished is an area in which the church has frequently missed the boat, yet it's an incredible opportunity to extend the kind of mercy that the outside world cannot comprehend. Not to mention, Jesus flat out said, "But when you give a banquet, invite the poor, the crippled, the lame, the blind, and you will be blessed. Although they cannot repay you, you will be repaid at the resurrection of the righteous" (Luke 14:13–14).

Dr. Allen Ross does a great job of nailing down why merciful people are blessed: "They are called blessed because they place showing mercy above their own rights; they take no hostile stand against people in need, but try to show kindness to others and heal wounds. It is not that they are merciful by nature, but because they have been shown mercy and live in constant dependence on the Lord."[5] This sounds a lot like what Jesus said in the parable of the sheep and the goats.

> When the Son of Man comes in his glory, and all the angels with him, he will sit on his glorious throne. All the nations will be gathered before him, and he will separate the people one from another as a shepherd separates the

sheep from the goats. He will put the sheep on his right and the goats on his left.

Then the King will say to those on his right, "Come, you who are blessed by my Father; take your inheritance, the kingdom prepared for you since the creation of the world. For I was hungry and you gave me something to eat, I was thirsty and you gave me something to drink, I was a stranger and you invited me in, I needed clothes and you clothed me, I was sick and you looked after me, I was in prison and you came to visit me."

Then the righteous will answer him, "Lord, when did we see you hungry and feed you, or thirsty and give you something to drink? When did we see you a stranger and invite you in, or needing clothes and clothe you? When did we see you sick or in prison and go to visit you?"

The King will reply, "Truly I tell you, whatever you did for one of the least of these brothers and sisters of mine, you did for me."

Then he will say to those on his left, "Depart from me, you who are cursed, into the eternal fire prepared for the devil and his angels. For I was hungry and you gave me nothing to eat, I was thirsty and you gave me nothing to drink, I was a stranger and you did not invite me in, I needed clothes and you did not clothe me, I was sick and in prison and you did not look after me."

They also will answer, "Lord, when did we see you hungry or thirsty or a stranger or needing clothes or sick or in prison, and did not help you?"

He will reply, "Truly I tell you, whatever you did not do for one of the least of these, you did not do for me."

> Then they will go away to eternal punishment, but the righteous to eternal life. (Matt. 25:31–46)

Again, we are not to be merciful in order to earn our salvation—our debt has already been paid. Rather, our mercy toward others is to be a visible response to the gratitude for that debt.

Blessed Are the Pure in Heart

Jesus goes on, "Blessed are the pure in heart, for they will see God" (5:8). To have purity of heart is to pursue God over anything else in our lives—over our kids, our marriages, our friendships, our careers, our comforts, our desires and even our Netflix binge-watching addictions.

The goal of the pure in heart is to align their lives with the truth of God's Word and to intentionally fight against anything that would distract them from doing God's will. The condition of our hearts is referenced 570 times in the New International Version of the Bible,[6] so this is obviously very important to God. The only others words more frequently used are "God," "Lord" and "Father."

We also know that the single-minded pursuit of a pure heart was important to Jesus, because He said it was the greatest commandment. "Jesus replied: 'Love the Lord your God with all your heart and with all your soul and with all your mind.' This is the first and greatest commandment" (22:37–38).

Jesus was quoting the Old Testament in this verse (see Deut. 6:5), drawing from a passage in which Moses was teaching the Israelites the Ten Commandments that the Lord had given him. Moses was instructing the people to impress the commandments on their children, to talk about them, to tie them around their wrists, to paint them on their gates and doorframes—basically always to have them on their minds. Being pure in heart is pretty important to the Lord, important enough for Jesus to include it as a characteristic of a blessed life.

Jesus was well aware of God's game plan regarding His death and resurrection, and He wanted to make it crystal clear that He was not giving up His life in exchange for reformed behavior and lists of rules on our part. A group of people had already nailed that role—they were called the Pharisees. And this is what Jesus thought of their changed actions but unchanged hearts: "Woe to you, teachers of the law and Pharisees, you hypocrites! You are like whitewashed tombs, which look beautiful on the outside but on the inside are full of the bones of the dead and everything unclean" (Matt. 23:27).

No, Jesus has never been concerned with how the picture looks on the outside—He has always wanted the heart! Actions alone do not change the condition of a heart, but a changed heart does lead to changed actions. That is why Jesus has no problem using people to initiate radical movements who, from the outside, appear dirty, messy and flawed. How do we become people with purified hearts? The first step is committing to follow Christ and His teachings—our initial salvation.

This beatitude promises that the pure in heart will see God. But unless we become pure in heart by following through with Romans 10:9 ("If you declare with your mouth, 'Jesus is Lord,' and believe in your heart that God raised him from the dead, you will be saved"), we will not experience the eternal benefits of seeing God.

This is the very truth Jesus was trying to get across to Nicodemus in John 3, when He told Nicodemus that no one could enter the kingdom of God unless he was born again. As Nicodemus wrestled with this concept, Jesus spoke the words that became probably the most well-known Bible verse in history, John 3:16: "God so loved the world that he gave his one and only Son, that whoever believes in him shall not perish but have eternal life."

Unfortunately, committing to follow Christ does not ensure that we will never sin again. The path to a pure heart is a continual process. One way that we can purify our hearts is to remove distractions that take our focus away from God. This is challenging in a culture that seems to make the pursuit of pleasure and possessions the purpose of life.

But an unbridled American dream deprives us of the single-minded pursuit of God. When we remove our focus from using our gifts and talents to build His kingdom, we instead produce an inward focus that results in building our own kingdoms.

When I was younger, I rode and showed horses, and every year I rode my horse in our little town's parade to kick off the rodeo season. (I feel an overwhelming amount of embarrassment about telling you this because it confirms every stereotype ever made about someone from Houston, Texas.)

I would put blinders on my horse during the parade route; this would restrict his peripheral vision and force him to stay focused on what was in front of him. This was needed because, between the marching bands, cheering crowds and emergency vehicles along the parade route, my horse could easily get distracted and unintentionally do something that would harm both of us.

A horse wearing blinders is a perfect illustration of being pure in heart. We need to be intentional about filtering out distractions so we can see the Lord working right in front of us. For me, putting on blinders meant making a commitment to get out from under the things that entangled my family; it meant being a real illustration of the gospel to our community and world.

By the time my husband and I had been married eight years, I was pregnant with our third child, we owned a four-bedroom home that was larger than any home my husband had ever lived in while growing up, and we were $80,000 in debt.

We had fallen into the trap that so many others of our generation have fallen into: we thought that we needed to be at the same standard of living right out of college that our parents had reached after twenty years of working.

From the outside, we looked like the perfect suburban family—two kids with one on the way, an SUV sitting in the driveway, a playground set in the backyard, a great house and a stable marriage.

Nothing is wrong with this picture; but what Chad and I had done to gain all those things completely distracted us from being able to help anyone but ourselves. If we had wanted to take even the smallest steps toward being pure in heart, we wouldn't have had the capacity to do so at that time.

Looking at our financial situation, we knew we needed to do something radical, or we would be in real trouble in the near future. So a few months before having our son, we sold our house and moved into a rental almost half the size. We sold our SUV, had multiple garage sales to sell most of what we owned and began to aggressively pay off our debt.

Our motive was simply to get control of our finances, but this process opened our eyes to the grip that our possessions had on us and brought us to that moment of crisis when we realized that God wanted total ownership of our lives and resources. The Lord has not always called us to such radical acts; sometimes the most beautiful picture of obedience is found in following the Lord in small acts every day. But sometimes we need something over-the-top radical to convince ourselves that we are all in.

The most interesting part of those years of transition was the comments people made to us. They said things like, "Did Chad lose his job?" or "Be sure to put an alarm in your rental house; that's a rough neighborhood." (I can assure you that it was not; it only had one park instead of five, but my kids survived just fine.)

We even had someone accuse my husband of not keeping his family safe because we sold our SUV and purchased a more affordable, smaller car. But we put blinders on, and we slowly stripped away the distractions one at a time.

In two years we were completely debt-free. In year three we gave away 40 percent of our income and became actively involved in orphan prevention and care, as well as the fight against child trafficking.

I love how the promise in this beatitude is that those who are pure in heart will see God. Outside of seeing Him in eternity, the closest we can get to seeing God here on earth is by loving people the way He does, and that is exactly what my family got to do.

The times when I have seen God the most clearly were the times when I have cleared my heart from all distractions and pursued Him with single-minded focus.

True Satisfaction

Our human desire to be part of something larger than ourselves is good—in fact, it is God-given. We just need to remember that it can never be satisfied with possessions, people or religious checklists. Despite the seeming paradox, our desire for purpose and meaning is fulfilled only when we empty ourselves of all our own desires and efforts, and allow God to fill us up with Himself and His will for our lives.

When we sense that dissatisfaction inside us, we need to let it drive us to an increasingly deeper relationship with Christ. That's why it's there!

As we seek God's kingdom and learn to love what matters to Him, we will bring Him glory and find the satisfaction we so long for.

5

A Higher Standard

If you've ever played sports or been in any kind of competition, you've probably been pushed by a coach or teacher to run faster, jump higher, hold on longer or do better than you thought you could. Sometimes this kind of pressure can be frustrating or even overwhelming, but we all know deep inside that it's for our best.

One of my CrossFit coaches, Alli, is by far the most optimistic person I have met in my entire life! I think she honestly believes that my body is capable of doing the same things as Olympic athletes' bodies, based on the activities she is always talking me into trying—activities any normal person would claim impossible after taking one look at me. One time she talked me into doing a WOD ("Workout of the Day") called "Murph." It consisted of a one-mile run, one hundred pull-ups, two hundred push-ups, three hundred squats and another one-mile run—all on the clock.

When my gym had sign-ups for this workout, I signed up to do it with a partner so I could split it with someone. Well, Alli got wind of this and began applying her powerful skills of persuasion, pushing me to do the workout solo—as in all by myself! I gave way to her urging; and fifty-nine minutes and forty-six seconds after starting the workout, I completed it.

Every time I tried to walk the next week I looked more like a newborn giraffe attempting to walk for the first time than a functioning human being, but I was never more proud of my fitness level. Without Alli's push that day to go for it, I would not have had the confidence to complete that workout or the two CrossFit competitions I've completed since then.

Jesus asks the same thing of His followers. Not only does He ask us to do the incredibly hard task of emptying ourselves, He goes even further and asks us to do things that, to our natural senses, seem impossible. Actually, what He asks us to do seems downright unreasonable in some cases—like when He says we should love our enemies and hate our family. Wait, what? (See Luke 14:26.)

This path to true blessing seems pretty radical, but just as the sweat and labor of athletic or artistic training pay off in rewards, so does our willingness to come up to the high bar that Jesus sets for His followers.

Blessed Are the Peacemakers

As a society, we are truly terrible peacemakers. But this quality is another aspect of a truly blessed life: "Blessed are the peacemakers, for they will be called children of God" (Matt. 5:9). The development of social media has not helped in this area—at all! Social media gives us this false sense of privacy in a very public forum. We are able to hide our faces behind a computer screen or mobile device, but once we hit "post," our opinions, feelings and souls are out for all the Internet to see. Not so private anymore—and way too often, not at all peaceable.

When Chad and I were going through adoption education classes, we were encouraged to make sure that anything we posted online about our adopted child would be honoring and respectful of her story, because one day our child would Google her name and read everything we wrote about her. This is true for social media in general; our kids will one day have social media of their own, and they will have access to everything we posted. We need to keep that in mind next time we are tempted to go on a social media tirade.

But it's not just social media. We flip on the TV, and not only is it hard to find any peacemakers, but the quest for higher ratings and more fans drives people to act a fool to get some TV time. Take reality TV, for example. The most popular reality TV stars are many times the ones who wage the most war. Our culture is obsessed with conflict and estranged relationships.

Some people even intentionally seek out conflict, although most of us are more ambiguous in our discord. (Side note: If you are just getting to know someone and, as my friend Melysa says, "trying to figure out if you want a second date," and the person describes himself as someone who can't stand drama, you can be assured that drama follows that person around like a bad storm. Only people who are immersed in drama point out how much they hate it! End side note.)

Conflict is the complete opposite of God's interests; He gave His very Son in order to reconcile each one of us to relationship with Him. That is why this beatitude says that peacemakers will be called children of God. Children take on the characteristics of their parents, and God is the ultimate peacemaker.

Peacemakers don't have to tell people that they are peacemakers (as is true with most genuine characteristics); they just show it through their actions.

Unfortunately, that means the opposite is also true—our actions can also indicate that we aren't interested in seeking out peace. In Matthew 5:38–47, Jesus set some pretty specific standards about how we should relate to others.

> You have heard that it was said, "Eye for eye, and tooth for tooth." But I tell you, do not resist an evil person. If anyone slaps you on the right cheek, turn to them the other cheek also. And if anyone wants to sue you and take your shirt, hand over your coat as well. If anyone forces you to go one mile, go with them two miles. Give to the one who asks you, and do not turn away from the one who wants to borrow from you.
>
> You have heard that it was said, "Love your neighbor and hate your enemy." But I tell you, love your enemies and pray for those who persecute you, that you may be children of your Father in heaven. He causes his sun to rise on the evil and the good, and sends rain on the righteous and the unrighteous. If you love those who love you, what reward will you get? Are not even the tax collectors doing that? And if you greet only your own people, what are you doing more than others? Do not even pagans do that?

What an incredibly high standard—and isn't that really the point? We can't go too far in making efforts to be peaceful. Peacemakers have no room for being passive-aggressive and immature; rather, they respond to conflict in ways that go beyond what anyone expects. We also see in this passage that it is not our responsibility to fight back but to trust the Lord with that role: "He causes his sun to rise on the evil and the good, and sends rain on the righteous and the unrighteous" (Matt. 5:45).

How do we become peacemakers? One simple but powerful way is found, plain as day, right in the middle of the passage we just read: we pray for our enemies. It can be incredibly hard to go to the throne of God on behalf of someone we hate or someone who has cut us deeply and shaken us to our core. It takes a huge amount of vulnerability and self-reflection to lift that person up in prayer.

But praying for our enemies is as much for us as it is for them—maybe even *more* for us. When we ask God to bless and reveal truth to someone who represents to us feelings of hate, anger and bitterness, the Holy Spirit begins to remove the chains that so tightly wrap around our hearts.

We begin to realize that our refusal to make peace never hurts our enemies in the first place; all it does is put a wedge between us and God.

Half the battle in praying for our enemies is just starting. When I don't know what to say or how to begin, I don't try to come up with something on my own; I pray the Lord's Prayer. It sounds a little something like this:

> Our Father in heaven, hallowed be Your name, Your kingdom come, Your will be done, on earth as it is in heaven. Give [______________] today [his or her] daily bread. And forgive [______________ his or her] debts, as I also [ask You to help me] forgive [______________]. And lead [______________] not into temptation, but deliver [______________] from the evil one. (Adapted from Matt. 6:9–13.)

At times, I have had to say that prayer over and over again, until I began to feel my chains loosening a little bit more every time I said it.

Nothing we could say while praying for our enemies will be a surprise to God; He already knows how we feel toward that person and what is in our hearts. We need to give ourselves the freedom to say it aloud, and we need to give God the opportunity to work.

A second way we can become peacemakers is to address people with whom we have conflicts before disagreements escalate. At the slightest hint of conflict, commit to making peace before things have a chance to get explosive.

The longer we wait to address a situation, the harder it is to talk ourselves into making peace. Now this is not a free ticket for us to fly off the handle and call someone out in the middle of an argument—that's called wreaking havoc, not making peace. Sometimes the best contribution we can make toward peace is to shut our mouth, take a time-out and cool down.

But once we have cooled down, we should address the situation as soon as we can and not allow Satan room to ignite disunity or bitterness. This is exactly what Paul was getting at in Romans when he said, "If it is possible, as far as it depends on you, live at peace with everyone" (12:18).

We are sinful, flawed human beings trying to coexist with other sinful, flawed human beings. We are going to hurt and damage each other; but when this happens, responding to our hurt in a spiritually mature way gives us a chance to make God look good to the outside world. Here are some ways to be spiritually mature:

- As far as it depends on you, don't be passive-aggressive.
- As far as it depends on you, start a conversation with someone about whom you feel conflicted.
- As far as it depends on you, don't immediately go to another aisle at the grocery store when you spot someone who has offended you.
- As far as it depends on you, extend forgiveness.

However, Paul does not say, "As far as it depends on you, set yourself up for a hurtful situation again in the future," or "As far as it depends on you, spend every moment with the person who has hurt you trying to rekindle the relationship."

John Piper says it like this: "We pray and we take whatever practical initiatives we can to make peace beginning with something as simple as a greeting. But we do not always succeed. And I want to make sure you don't equate peacemaking with peace-achieving. A peacemaker longs for peace, and works for peace, and sacrifices for peace. But the attainment of peace may not come."[1]

The goal is to be sure that we can walk away from a situation or relationship and ask ourselves, "Did I do everything I could to make peace?"

If we become peacemakers, not only will our relationships be healthier and our hearts purer, but we will be called the very children of God. But why is that? What is it about peace that makes us heirs of God?

We have already seen how God, by sending Jesus to reconcile us to Himself, extended the ultimate gift of peace—the life of His Son. When we extend peace to others, we are called children of God, because we reflect the characteristics of our Father.

Blessed Are the Persecuted and Insulted

Jesus intentionally ended with two beatitudes on persecution because He knew that pursuing the truly blessed life would result in opposition.

> Blessed are those who are persecuted because of righteousness, for theirs is the kingdom of heaven. Blessed are you when people insult you, persecute you and falsely say all kinds of evil against you because of me. Rejoice and be glad, because great is your reward in heaven, for in the same way they persecuted the prophets who were before you. (Matt. 5:10–12)

But why is this? How can someone who relies on Jesus; mourns over his own sin and the sin of others; and is meek, righteous, merciful, pure in heart and peaceful be persecuted? What could such a person possibly do to offend anyone? Well, such a person's lifestyle convicts others. It displays the stark reality of truth against people's love of what is false.

When I was in high school, my friends and I played a game called "Bowl of Death," or "BOD" for short. Everyone received three slips of paper and wrote any question they wanted. All of the questions went into a bowl, and as the bowl was passed around, each person pulled out a question and had to answer it. We took this game seriously and often played for hours.

Why, yes, I was superpopular in high school. I mean, how could I not be when my Friday nights consisted of being locked up in my room playing BOD with my other superpopular friends? I know, I know, what does this have to do with persecution? Well, as we got older, my friends and I still got together on college breaks and played a rousing game of BOD for old times' sake. But the questions started to change, mainly because when you play a divulge-every-part-of-your-soul kind of game every weekend for six straight years, you only have so much left to ask.

The questions started to take on more of a philosophical approach—the kinds of questions most college-age people wrestle with: "What would you do in __________ situation?" or "Do you think God would be okay with ______________ if He knew it was for a good reason?" or even the more intense "Do you think God really allows people to go to hell?"

The interesting thing is that, despite our close relationships, as our questions about life became more intense and the reality of God's Word harder for us to accept, at times it caused a disconnect in our friendships, because the reality of God's Word is challenging.

Sometimes Jesus' answers to these questions are crystal clear, but sometimes they aren't. Sometimes they are messy and vague; and, to be completely honest, we don't always like them.

At times truth gets uncomfortable, and it can be easier to just believe something else. So when we continue to fight for truth and try to redefine concepts like blessings, we can run into persecution.

We find a great illustration of Jesus experiencing this with the Pharisees. He said to them, "No one can serve two masters. Either you will hate the one and love the other, or you will be devoted to the one and despise the other. You cannot serve both God and money" (Luke 16:13).

Then came the persecution, the mockery: "The Pharisees, who loved money, heard all this and were sneering at Jesus" (16:14). Why the criticism? Because Jesus' attitude toward money was an attack on the Pharisees' attitude toward money. But Jesus didn't let persecution stop Him from pursuing the truth; rather He said, "You are the ones who justify yourselves in the eyes of others, but God knows your hearts. What people value highly is detestable in God's sight" (Luke 16:15).

At the core of persecution is the contrast of truth against the love of a lie. If we are walking through our lives without, at the very least, some raised eyebrows or judgmental questioning, we need to take some time to consider whether our faith lines up with the faith of believers in the New Testament. Do our lives look different from the people in the world around us? Would we describe our lives as blessed?

Two years ago, when I finally reached the end of my efforts to live by a checklist, my family set out on a journey to redefine a blessed life. That journey has taken us from paying off $80,000 of debt, to fighting vicious injustices like poverty and child sex trafficking, to bringing home our fourth child from the poorest province in China.

Along the way we have had critics; we have doubted (and continue to fight doubt); and we have been called crazy, irresponsible and poor providers for our family. We have been told that we need to calm down, settle in and think about our financial future.

But I hope we are just getting started, because I have never been more fulfilled and full of joy in all my life, and I absolutely would do every part of this transition all over again. I pray that God will give us the opportunity to continue to chase breathlessly after Him and to confuse those around us for many, many years to come.

Unfortunately, the harshest words ever spoken to or about my family are nothing compared to the persecution that many of our brothers and sisters in Christ experience all over the world. An organization called Open Doors works in the world's most oppressive countries to empower Christians who are persecuted for their beliefs.

Open Doors equips persecuted Christians in more than sixty countries through such programs as Bible and gospel development, women and children advancement, and Christian community restoration. The Open Doors website features story after story of Christians all over the world who are being persecuted, some even by their immediate family, and many who are being killed. Churches are ransacked, and children are kidnapped or tortured as a result of their parents' faith in Jesus. Women are raped, beaten and exploited because they refuse to denounce Christ.

Here is one of the stories from the field:

> For Batima [her name is changed for protection], a college student in Kyrgyzstan, Christ's words in John 15:20 have proven to be true since she came to faith in Him a year ago: "If they persecuted me, they will persecute you also." When she was invited by her family for a visit, she could never have guessed what awaited her. Intent on forcing her to renounce her newfound faith, her own brothers and sister brutally beat her until she sustained a concussion and lost consciousness. They then tied her up and took her phone and personal documents.
>
> She somehow found the strength to escape, and is now in hiding, where she has received basic treatment for her wounds. Despite the pain of Batima's recovery, our field worker reports that she is in good spirits.[2]

This type of persecution is more in alignment with what Jesus was referring to in the Beatitudes than what we typically experience in America, because He was well aware of the road ahead for His disciples and those who would follow Him in the future.

Yet, despite the atrocities that can be attributed to persecution, Jesus says, "Rejoice and be glad, because great is your reward in heaven, for in the same way they persecuted the prophets who were before you" (Matt. 5:12).

But how do we do that? How do we rejoice and be glad during times of persecution? Well, Jesus outlines three clear ways to train ourselves to be people of gladness during persecution. Note specifically the word "train," because being glad under pressure is a learned attitude in partnership with the Holy Spirit. Rejoicing during times of discomfort is not something that comes naturally to us.

First, rewards are powerful. Right after Jesus says "Rejoice and be glad," He gives us the reason that we can rejoice and be glad: "because great is your reward in heaven." Rewards have always been and always will be a powerful motivation of action and behavior in human beings. All we need to do is spend thirty minutes around any child, and we will see how powerful a tool reward can be. Jesus knew that to be true for us as well.

This reward is, in fact, the reward of heaven, because Jesus said that those who are persecuted will receive the blessing of "the kingdom of heaven" (5:10). But the reward goes further than that, because Jesus says next in verse 12 that those who are persecuted because of Him will reap a "great . . . reward" on the other side of eternity.

We don't know completely what that reward will be, since we have yet to go to heaven; but even if we did know, we likely couldn't totally understand its enormity. I believe that when we get to heaven, those with the most adorned crowns will be people we have never heard of, people who served God faithfully despite persecution but never sought or received earthly recognition, because they looked to the "great . . . reward in heaven."

Second, a heavenly mind-set is powerful. If we fully understood the perfection that is heaven, the reward of heaven alone would be enough for us. None of us can describe heaven, but we do get a pretty good idea of what it is going to be like through various passages in Scripture. This one is by far my favorite:

> Then I saw "a new heaven and a new earth," for the first heaven and the first earth had passed away, and there was no longer any sea. I saw the Holy City, the new Jerusalem, coming down out of heaven from God, prepared as a bride beautifully dressed for her husband. And I heard a loud voice from the throne saying, "Look! God's dwelling place is now among the people, and he will dwell with them. They will be his people, and God himself will be with them and be their God. 'He will wipe every tear from their eyes. There will be no more death or mourning or crying or pain,' for the old order of things has passed away."
>
> He who was seated on the throne said, "I am making everything new!" Then he said, "Write this down, for these words are trustworthy and true."
>
> He said to me: "It is done. I am the Alpha and the Omega, the Beginning and the End. To the thirsty I will give water without cost from the spring of the water of life. Those who are victorious will inherit all this, and I will be their God and they will be my children. But the cowardly, the unbelieving, the vile, the murderers, the sexually immoral,

> those who practice magic arts, the idolaters and all liars—they will be consigned to the fiery lake of burning sulfur. This is the second death." (Rev. 21:1–8)

Imagine a place in which there is no pain, only joy; no sadness, only rejoicing; no death, only life; no poverty, only fullness; no evil, only love—and then think about the fact that a place just like this is our inheritance, because we are the children of God. One way to rejoice and be glad in any trying situation, especially persecution, is to focus on eternity.

Third, the remembrance of history is powerful. Jesus said, "In the same way they persecuted the prophets who were before you" (Matt. 5:12). Jesus is essentially saying that we are not the first to be persecuted for choosing a life that reflects His definition of blessed, and we won't be the last.

The encouraging part of this is that it reminds us of the spiritual giants who have gone before us, those who have set an extraordinary example of how to be glad and rejoice in times of persecution. Jesus is encouraging us to look at their example when persecution is overwhelming.

We have people like Stephen (stoned to death, see Acts 6:8–15; 7:54–60), Andrew (crucified), Simon Peter (crucified upside down so as to not be executed in the same way as Jesus), William Tyndale (choked to death while tied to a stake and then burned), Dietrich Bonhoeffer (hung in a concentration camp), Jim Elliot (slaughtered in Ecuador by the people he was ministering to), and the list could go on and on.

While we can look to them for encouragement, we too have the chance to set an example for the next generation of Christ followers, should the Lord ever find us worthy of being on such a list.[3]

A Different Kind of Blessing

The reason the Beatitudes are so countercultural is that they were not written just for our earthly existence. Sure, aligning our lives with the Beatitudes will indeed produce a blessed life unlike one we have ever experienced before, but that is just half the blessing. The other half will be fulfilled on the other side of eternity—a heavenly blessing.

C.S. Lewis described this best: "If I find in myself a desire which no experience in this world can satisfy, the most probable explanation is that I was made for another world."[4] The American dream has essentially redefined a blessed life to reflect things of the here and now and oftentimes feeds a self-centric mind-set.

Yet Jesus outlined a blessed life that focuses on growing His kingdom here on earth and continues into our eternal life. This is exactly what He meant when He said, "Do not store up for yourselves treasures on earth, where moths and vermin destroy, and where thieves break in and steal. But store up for yourselves treasures in heaven, where moths and vermin do not destroy, and where thieves do not break in and steal. For where your treasure is, there your heart will be also" (Matt. 6:19–21).

What if, instead of praying for the blessings of more money, the promotion, the larger house on the corner or whatever it is for each of us, we turned our prayers toward heaven and asked for a different kind of blessing? The kind that involves being transformed into a person who reflects a life that is poor in spirit, meek, righteous, merciful, pure in heart, peaceful and glad in the face of persecution.

What if our blessings couldn't be defined in visible items that could be posted on social media but, rather, in blessings such as comfort, mercy, inheritance and even heaven? What if we said "no" to society defining our life as blessed or successful and said "yes" to the things of Jesus?

What would our marriages look like? How would our friendships change? What difference would we make in our communities? What freedom would we receive? Jesus is calling—how will we answer?

Don't be too blessed to say "yes."

6

Moment of Truth

I almost feel as if I need to give a disclaimer to this chapter, something like, "Proceed at your own risk," but then I would be like one of those Christian T-shirt shops that sell items with cheesy slogans and logos. But in fair warning, this chapter contains ideas that get in our face and make us feel a little bit uncomfortable—okay, maybe a lot uncomfortable. Some messages, despite our best efforts to sugarcoat them or soften the presentation, are just tough to hear, and we can't change that. The passage we are going to look at in this chapter is one of those.

Billy Sunday, a fiery twentieth-century baseball player turned evangelist, summed up why the Bible is so challenging to us; his words ring particularly true regarding this passage, especially for those of us living in suburban America: "The reason you don't like the Bible, you old sinner, is because it knows all about you."[1]

Thank you for those encouraging words, Billy. But he is right—rarely, if ever, do we read a book that seems to know and address all the worst parts of us, and yet tells us how loved we are with the turn of every page. Just because we are Christians, however, doesn't mean we like everything we read in the Bible.

Just the other day, I said to God in response to a passage I was reading, "You don't really mean that, do You, God?" But I pray that we are always challenged by the Word of God, because He is still God, and we are still being refined. So let's tackle this passage with an open mind-set of getting comfortable with being uncomfortable.

In three chapters of the New Testament, we come across one of the most awkward exchanges in the Bible—one that took place between Jesus and a man who had a great deal of wealth. This story about a rich young ruler can be found in Matthew 19:16–30, Mark 10:17–31 and Luke 18:18–30). The Mark account of this passage is my favorite, so that is the one we are going to study.

I have struggled with this passage my entire life, and though the struggle has been less real in the last couple of years, it is still something I must keep at the forefront of my mind, because I am still learning lessons about the rich and the kingdom of God. So let's look at key insights in each verse throughout this passage and then dive into some modern-day applications.

Getting to the Heart of the Matter

Right off the bat Mark begins to pull at our heartstrings by describing this young man's reaction to Jesus. The young man ran up to Jesus and fell on his knees. "'Good teacher,' he asked, 'what must I do to inherit eternal life?'" (Mark 10:17).

Think about all the wealthy people you have ever known (maybe personally or even just through the media). Have any of them ever come across to you as the type who would be so desperate as to beg for something? This is not a sweeping stereotype of all wealthy people—I have known some truly humble wealthy people—but in many cases people work hard to become wealthy not just to be financially secure, but also to be free of accountability and dependence on others. This is another dangerous trick of the American dream—the line of thought that we have really made it when we become our own boss!

People don't typically work hard to be successful so that they can find themselves groveling at someone's feet but, rather, so that they can be free of submission to anyone else.

But this man did not seem to struggle with that, at least not in front of Jesus. I'm not sure if he totally believed that Jesus was the Son of God, but he obviously believed that Jesus had the answers to eternal life and the authority to tell him how to get that life. So much so that when he saw Jesus walking away, he had a "now or never" reaction and ran up to Jesus and fell before Him, immediately putting himself in a position of surrender and adoration.

So here we are reading along, and perhaps we are thinking, *Man, this guy really loves Jesus! I bet Jesus is about to pull one of those "Your faith has saved you; go in peace" moves like He did in Luke 7:50. I mean, the man even complimented Jesus when he asked Him how to have eternal life!* But that's not what happened.

The man called Jesus "good teacher," but why? Well, at first thought we might think it's because he was talking to Jesus—of course Jesus was good; actually, He was perfect. Yet the way this man asked the question quickly indicates that He believed salvation to be a reflection of works, and he thought Jesus was really nailing it in the "good works" department, you know, with the miracles and all.

The man didn't call Jesus "good" because he believed that He was "good" for saving us and offering His life so that we would not get what we deserve. This man didn't know that any of that was about to go down. The man called Jesus good because of all that he had heard through the grapevine that Jesus had done up until that point.

Because Jesus and God are One (see John 10:30), Jesus could see what was going on in the mind and heart of this young man. In other words, Jesus knew the why behind the man's question, and that may be the single most important thing to keep in mind as we study this passage.

Jesus responds in verses 18–19 of Mark 10: "Why do you call me good? . . . No one is good—except God alone." This response had to have thrown the guy off a bit. Jesus, who was perfect, had just said that even He wasn't good. Why would He do that? Why would Jesus point out that only God is good, indirectly saying that He was not good?

Jesus was not trying to disprove His divinity; He was pointing out that it is impossible for anyone to be good enough to inherit eternal life, that only God is truly good, and we aren't Him. But just in case that didn't get across to this guy, Jesus then listed some of what we know as the Ten Commandments. You may notice that Jesus only listed the commandments that have to do with how we should treat others—no murder, no adultery, no lying, no jealousy and be sure to honor your parents. He left off some key commandments like putting nothing before God and worshiping Him alone, and not because he couldn't recall all the commandments. Jesus knew exactly what He was doing. He was setting the man up to reply a certain way: "'Teacher,' he declared, 'all these I have kept since I was a boy'" (Mark 10:20).

This is a seriously impressive accomplishment. This young man had gone his entire life not murdering or cheating on his wife—okay, maybe this part is not that outstanding, a lot of people have avoided these sins. But going his entire life never lying, being jealous or dishonoring his parents—that's amazing!

We can't hear the tone of the man's voice, but his response to Jesus was probably not one of pride. We already know that he wasn't too prideful to fall at the feet of Jesus, so he wasn't pointing out that he had followed all these from the time he was a child in order to convey a "Look at me, I'm killing it" type attitude.

We can likely read his response as one of disappointment, because he had probably been hoping that Jesus would give him an answer that was different from the list he had been checking off his entire life. He needed it to be different, because that list had left him wondering about eternal life, had left him discontent, had left him yearning for more.

That list had been exhausting. Turns out I'm not the first person to try and spend my entire life making a pretty impressive checklist—this guy had been doing it long before I was around.

But Jesus knew his heart and his struggle, and He drew him into saying, "All these I have kept since I was a boy." He wanted this interaction to make an impression on the young man. He wanted to get to his heart. Before telling us Jesus' response to the rich young ruler's statement, Mark gives us an inside look into what Jesus was feeling toward this man: "Jesus looked at him and loved him" (Mark 10:21). Jesus didn't give him an "Oh, bless your sweet heart, you are trying really hard, aren't you?" kind of look but an "I need you to understand that this is about more than your actions; I want your heart" kind of look.

What the rich young ruler didn't know was that Jesus did have a way that he had never considered before, but it could not be contained in any sort of list. "'One thing you lack,' he said. 'Go, sell everything you have and give to the poor, and you will have treasure in heaven. Then come, follow me'" (10:21).

It is really important that we know Jesus' heart behind this, because we could easily think that He was asking this man to reconcile his works-driven mind-set with more works. That's exactly what Jesus did, right? He told the man to sell everything, give it to the poor and follow Him. Well, He did and He didn't, all at the same time.

For those of us who are parents, we sometimes ask our children to do things that are less about the actions themselves and more about what the actions indicate about their hearts. Recently Chad and I took our three oldest kids to the movies so that Pixar would yet again control their minds while taking all our money. Now, I don't ever go to the movies without buying Nestle's Buncha Crunch candy (little pieces of crunchy goodness covered in chocolate and stuck together with other little pieces of goodness), and I have passed this tradition down to my children as well. (I don't know the last time you bought refreshments at the movies for four children, but it costs roughly what an entire semester of college tuition would.)

When we got to our theater, it was still being cleaned. While we waited outside, I noticed a little girl (maybe five years old) eyeing my kids with all their candy, so I said to my daughter, "Why don't you offer that little girl some of your candy? But make sure to ask her parents first." I didn't necessarily ask my daughter to do that because I thought she had too much candy (I had just bought all that for her!), but I asked her to do it because it is a good practice for her to give and especially to give things she may prefer to keep. But it's also a good indication to me of what is more important to her heart: candy or people.

Jesus didn't tell this man to sell everything and follow Him because He was mad at the man for being wealthy; He told Him to do it because He knew that the idol of wealth had taken a front seat in this man's life. Based on the next part of the story, we know that Jesus was right: "At this the man's face fell. He went away sad, because he had great wealth" (Mark 10:22).

I wonder if the man was sad at the thought of losing all his wealth or disappointed in himself because he knew that he couldn't or wouldn't walk away from it all. Probably both.

A Teachable Moment

This next part is when it gets, well . . . awkward. The man had walked away; and for the first time since the conversation had started, Jesus looked around at His disciples who had been watching. Instead of just continuing on down the road, Jesus decided to make this a teachable moment for His disciples.

Now, we have to keep in mind that Jesus and His disciples were financially supported by the donations of Jesus' followers (as most ministries are today). But Jesus hadn't bent over backwards to accommodate this guy or make him feel good about himself just because he had a lot of money and could be a real game changer for Jesus' ministry bank account.

No, He'd been more interested in this guy's heart than his money. Jesus let the man just walk way—not at all a common thing for a religious leader to do with a wealthy person. The disciples must have been astonished enough at that, but Jesus' explanation of the matter really bewildered them.

The Lord turned to His disciples and said (rather intensely, might I add), "'How hard it is for the rich to enter the kingdom of God!' The disciples were amazed at his words. But Jesus said again, 'Children, how hard it is to enter the kingdom of God! It is easier for a camel to go through the eye of a needle than for someone who is rich to enter the kingdom of God'" (Mark 10:23–25).

Not really knowing how to respond (because, well, Jesus may have seemed a little frustrated) and perhaps murmuring to each other under their breath, one of them said, "Who then can be saved?" (10:26).

The disciples' amazement was probably mixed with shock, because they weren't dumb—they knew that it was impossible for a camel to go through the eye of a needle. Therefore Jesus seemed to be saying that it was impossible for a wealthy person to be saved. That immediately weeded out the most influential people in society—diplomats, politicians and even many religious people—everyone we would assume are shoo-ins for heaven. But not Jesus. Peter's response in the next couple of verses shows us that Jesus' words even led the disciples to question their own ability to inherit eternal life. But just as Jesus knew the rich young ruler's motive, He also knew the concern behind the disciples' question. "Jesus looked at them and said, 'With man this is impossible, but not with God; all things are possible with God'" (Mark 10:27).

Jesus wasn't saying, "Guys, no man can take a camel and shove it through the eye of a needle, but God could." Is God powerful enough that He could indeed manipulate the anatomy of a camel in such a way that it would fit through a needle? Sure. But that's not Jesus' point. He is saying that obedience means nothing if it is not partnered with a completely surrendered heart to God—and for people of privilege, that is an impossible place to get to on their own. It is only possible with God.

Peter spoke up next: "We have left everything to follow you!" (10:28). I love Peter. I can relate to a guy who reacts more than he thinks, is always the one to open his mouth (when everyone else is sure to be quiet), wants to be the best, needs some encouraging words every now and again, and always starts out strong but then ends by getting the proverbial hand slap. Bless him.

"'Truly I tell you,' Jesus replied, 'no one who has left home or brothers or sisters or mother or father or children or fields for me and the gospel will fail to receive a hundred times as much in this present age: homes, brothers, sisters, mothers, children and fields—along with persecutions—and in the age to come eternal life'" (10:29–30).

Jesus wanted His disciples to know that He and His Father in heaven were well aware of the sacrifices they had made to follow Him, but He also wanted to make sure they knew that following Him would not be without a cost, because He wanted His disciples to be prepared for the days to come.

He still desires that for His disciples today. It is not a question of *if* we will experience persecution because of following Jesus; it is a question of *when*. Thank goodness we already know that persecution is a characteristic of a blessed life!

True Reward

Jesus promised great reward in Mark 10:29–30 for those who gave up their treasures to follow Him; but before we head into application of this passage, it is important that we look also at what Jesus was *not* saying. It would be so easy to read these verses and think that Jesus was promising that for whatever we give, we will receive it back exactly—only a hundred times more.

Like, for every one dollar we give, we will receive one hundred dollars back. That is not at all what Jesus was saying. I mean, think about all that we have studied about the characteristics of a blessed life and generosity so far. Does this sound like something Jesus would say?

Jesus was not promoting any sort of prosperity gospel, which is simply the theological belief that it is God's will that Christians be wealthy (which some Christians believe) and that the more we give, the more we will receive (financially, anyway).

This belief is a slippery slope, because it simply doesn't apply to all contexts and cultures in which Christians around the world (including America) live.

A good friend of mine, Jen Hatmaker, said something that had a profound effect on me. (Okay, maybe we aren't friends—well, at least she doesn't know it yet; but should we ever meet one day, I can assure you that we would be the best of friends.) So, my good friend Jen Hatmaker said, "There is a biblical benchmark I now use. We will refer to this criterion for every hard question, big idea, topic, assessment of our own obedience, every 'should' or 'should not' and 'will' or 'will not' we ascribe to God, every theological sound bite. Here it is: If it isn't also true for a poor single Christian mom in Haiti, it isn't true."[2]

Is what Jesus asked of the rich young ruler something that He also asks of the Haitian woman in a village? Yes. Do the details of that request look different from one person to another? Sometimes. He is asking us not to allow anything to take precedent over following Him with our whole being. The reward Jesus refers to at the end of this passage is twofold. It is both present and eternal, much like the blessings outlined in the Beatitudes. However, when Jesus says that we will not "fail to receive a hundred times as much in this present age: homes, brothers, sisters, mothers, children and fields—along with persecutions—and in the age to come eternal life," He is talking not just about material blessings, but about the joy and happiness that comes from entering into Christian community. Now *that* applies to you, me and the Haitian woman in the village.

For example, if I went before my church and said that God had asked my family to sell everything we had and give it to the poor, we would receive one of two reactions. Some of our church attenders would invite us to come live with them and use one of their cars, donate clothes to our kids and feed us—they would meet all our immediate needs.

But others would call us foolish, irresponsible and reckless and would probably offer very little help to our family, because they would simply view our sudden need as consequences of our decision. It would not be easy by any means, but Jesus didn't say that to the rich young ruler or to His disciples; He just said that their sacrifice would be returned one hundred times over.

Jesus Doesn't Want Our Stuff–He Wants Our Hearts

Jesus ended His teaching with a nice, neat little bow on top: "But many who are first will be last, and the last first" (Mark 10:31). I, Jenny Jones, may have misquoted this verse no less than five thousand times while playing high school sports.

It was a great way to use God's Word to bring some humility to our winning opponents and also to make myself feel better about losing—you know, a real kill-two-birds-with-one-stone approach.

But seriously, our society tends to put those who have the most first, therefore putting those who have the least last. But that is the complete reverse of Jesus' order. This verse sums up the lesson that Jesus was trying to get across to the disciples and to us—our stuff, our wealth and even our status mean nothing if we aren't willing to use them to build God's kingdom and love people.

Interestingly, every time I have heard this story about the rich young ruler, it seems almost simultaneously to be followed by the sentence, "Now I don't think that God is telling us all to go out today and sell everything we own." It's almost as if it is important to give people a loophole because if we don't, they may not continue to listen. The teaching may be too hard, and people simply might not be ready for that.

But we can't just discredit the fact that Jesus is asking some people to sell everything and give it to the poor, just as He was of the rich young ruler. This is not an easy passage of Scripture to teach, especially in a suburban community like the one I live in. But the heart of the message is that God writes different stories in each of our lives; and while the story He is writing in yours or mine may or may not have the exact same details as that of the rich young ruler, it does have the same core truth: Jesus doesn't want just a part of your heart or mine—He wants all of it.

Our Own Rich-Young-Ruler Moments

Most of us, like the rich young ruler, have been faced with the kind of decision that forces all time to stand still—the kind of situation on which the entire course of our future hangs in the balance. Moments like these end up defining, influencing and outlining the much quieter and more subtle moments that occur during our everyday lives. However, the everyday moments are just as important, if not more important, than the defining ones, because over time the mundane decisions are the ones that determine the condition of our heart and our openness to God, and they prepare us to come face to face with the bigger fork-in-the-road decisions.

I have experienced the joy and the heartache of walking through these landmark moments in my own life, and I have watched loved ones and friends navigate them as well. Chad and I have come to lovingly refer to these as "rich-young-ruler moments," so much so that the phrase has become common terminology around the Jones household.

Many times, especially over the last couple of years, I have looked at my husband and said, "This is a rich-young-ruler moment. Whatever we decide needs to be what would bring the most glory to God and show people the most love."

We all have these rich-young-ruler moments—those moments when we get to the end of ourselves and run after Jesus, when we fall at His feet and ask, "What must I do to inherit eternal life?"

Those of us who are Christians and have declared with our mouths, "Jesus is Lord," and believed in our hearts "that God raised him from the dead" (Rom. 10:9) have already experienced our first rich-young-ruler moment—the one that started us down the road of following Jesus. But others before us had their own rich-young-ruler moments as well, and it was because of their decisions that we were led toward or away from Christ.

For example, when I was growing up, my parents did not make it a huge priority for our family to be active in church. However, my friend Sheryl's parents decided to make attending church a priority not only for their kids, but also for any other kids under their influence, and in God's sovereignty that is what He used to lead me to my first rich-young-ruler moment.

We don't know how the rest of the rich young ruler's life turned out, because Scripture never mentions him again. We have no idea how his life would have turned out if he had chosen to sell everything and follow Jesus—if, instead of walking away from Jesus, he had walked toward Jesus and away from his own wealth.

We would probably know a lot more about him than simply that he was a rich young ruler. We may have learned his actual name, which could have been listed with the likes of Peter, James or John.

One thing is for sure: we would not know him for what he wasn't willing to give up but, rather, for his absurd generosity and unwavering devotion to Christ. I suspect that because of his wealth, he probably walked away from his encounter with Jesus and continued to lead a safe, secure, good life, one that looked really successful from the outside and was probably even envied by most of the people he met—a life that by most standards was blessed. Sound familiar? The rich young ruler was literally too blessed to say "yes."

The rich young ruler is the reason that I am not a hoarder. I'm the opposite, actually—a disperser, if you will—and it drives my family crazy. We live under a strict policy: if you haven't used it in a year, get rid of it. At least once a week the following scenario plays out in our house.

Jones child #1 (while frantically looking for something): "Mom! I can't find __________!"

Jones child #2: "She probably donated it or sold it in the garage sale. It's gone."

I want a love of God over a love of materialism to be written into the DNA of my family. I don't ever want to walk away from anything the Lord is asking of us and, as a consequence, miss whatever God had in store for our lives. I don't want our stuff to cause us to live just a *good* life when we could live a *blessed* life! Not a blessed life as defined by our society, but one that reflects repentance, righteousness, purity, meekness, peace, mercy, simplicity—and the occasional run-in with persecution.

It is so easy for us to read this passage in Mark 10 and immediately jump to judgment of the rich young ruler. How could anyone look into the face of Jesus and walk away in disobedience?

But you and I do this more often than we would like to admit. I wish I could tell you that I have responded with unwavering faithfulness to every rich-young-ruler moment that has happened in my life, but the reality is that I haven't. Though we have not stared into the physical face of Jesus, we have seen His presence and provision enough to no longer excuse our distrust. When we say "no" to God or put Him in second place to anything, we aren't just being disobedient—we are saying that we don't trust the very Creator of the entire universe with the details of our lives.

Two years ago, at my point of spiritual crisis, I had to approach God and essentially ask for a do-over. It wasn't because I had ruined my life with an addiction or had a moral failure. My life had not hit rock bottom. I was a wife, a mom to three pretty awesome kids, and a pastor; my life actually looked pretty normal. But that's why I needed a do-over. I didn't want a normal life; I didn't want a life that reflected that of the rich young ruler. I wanted a life that said "*YES!*" As I read this passage during my six-month intensive on the New Testament, I didn't have any sort of moment right then. But I distinctly remember praying, "Lord, I don't know what my rich-young-ruler moment is going be, but when it happens, I say 'yes' to whatever it is. Please show me how to say 'yes.'"

He did. Enter Joseph of Arimathea and Zacchaeus.

7

Two Men Who Said "Yes"

It turns out that others in the Bible experienced rich-young-ruler moments. But some of those moments looked very different from the one we just studied. The rich young ruler said "no" and walked away from the fullness Jesus wanted him to have; but these other people said "yes" in the face of radical, life-changing opportunities. Two men in particular caught my attention: Joseph of Arimathea and Zacchaeus. These men said "yes" to the possibility of losing their jobs, public embarrassment, rejection and even giving up their identities. They said "yes" to being blessed. What was it that made them respond to Jesus differently than the rich young ruler? How did they understand that giving up everything would enable them to gain what really mattered? As I studied their lives, I found out—and I determined to follow their example.

The Rich-Young-Ruler Moment of Joseph of Arimathea

Despite the fact that he is described in all four Gospels (see Matt. 27:57–60; Mark 15:42–46; Luke 23:50–54; John 19:38–42),

Joseph of Arimathea is one of those people we could easily skim over in the New Testament. He is mentioned in only a few verses, but the impact he makes could fill an entire book.

Arimathea is not Joseph's last name. As with many people in biblical days, his second name simply indicated what town he was from, and it was also an easy way to distinguish one Joseph from another. Like the rich young ruler, Joseph was challenged with a defining moment after Jesus' crucifixion in which he had to make a quick decision that could cause him to ruin his reputation, lose his influence and even break Jewish law.

We are going to pull out significant parts of each Gospel account and retell a mashed-up version of the story. That being said, you may want to read each account of Joseph on your own, because each one is just as unique as the person writing the story.

Some facts we should know going into the story: Joseph of Arimathea was a rich man (see Matt. 27:57), which probably helped him gain his position on the Sanhedrin (see Mark 15:43; Luke 23:50), the supreme council of the Jewish people made up of chief priests, scribes, lawyers, older Jewish men and experts in Jewish law.[1] This was the same council led by Caiaphas, the chief priest who oversaw Jesus' case and ultimately advocated Jesus' crucifixion to Pilate.

But here is where things got sticky for Joseph. He was a disciple of Jesus, but he kept it secret "because he feared the Jewish leaders" (John 19:38). The Jewish leaders hated Jesus and were not shy about letting it be known. But Joseph was also described as "a good and upright man, who had not consented to their decision and action" (Luke 23:50–51).

Imagine being Joseph on the day Jesus was crucified. Here he was, a member of the very council that advocated crucifying the man he knew was the Son of God. At some point, Joseph had to have realized that there was nothing he could say or do to change Jesus' fate. The next thing he knew, Jesus was being nailed to a cross; and, despite his position, he had been unable to prevent it.

Here's where the story picks up. Jesus was crucified on what the Jewish people call a "preparation day" (the day before the Sabbath or before a holy festival). Because Joseph was on the Sanhedrin, he got word that Jesus had died quickly.

This was somewhat unexpected, not because Jesus was the Son of God and shouldn't have died, but because crucifixion was designed to be a particularly slow and excruciating death. It was a known fact that it could take days for someone to die by crucifixion. The Jewish people asked Pilate if they could break the legs of the three men who had been crucified that day to hasten their deaths so they would not be left to hang during the Sabbath (see John 19:31).

But when the soldiers went to break Jesus' legs, they discovered that He was already dead, and the prophecy that not one of Jesus' bones would be broken was fulfilled (see Ps. 34:20).

When Joseph got word of Jesus' death, he was faced with a rich-young-ruler moment. Because he was on the council, he was in a unique position to give Jesus a proper Jewish burial. This was not something that Jesus' disciples could do. Because of Jesus' radical claims that He would rise from the dead in three days, the disciples would not be allowed by the religious leaders to gain access to His body.

The disciples were also in hiding to some degree, because in their minds nothing was turning out as they had expected, and they feared that they too could be tried for blasphemy. No, this was something that only Joseph could do. As evening approached, Joseph knew that if he was going to do something, he needed to move quickly, because the Sabbath was just a few hours away. He faced a defining moment. The rest of the council had no idea that he was a believer in Jesus; Joseph could have decided that it was too risky to go behind Caiaphas' back to ask for Jesus' body.

He could have convinced himself that it was not his place or that it was the responsibility of those Jesus had been close to, but instead Joseph did something that only he was in a position to do—he *boldly* went to Pilate and asked for Jesus' body (see Mark 15:43).

Pilate's response? "Pilate was surprised to hear that he was already dead. Summoning the centurion, he asked him if Jesus had already died. When he learned from the centurion that it was so, he gave the body to Joseph" (15:44–45).

At this point Joseph was at another rich-young-ruler moment. Although he was a follower of Jesus, he was still Jewish and deeply cared about Jewish law (we know this because of how quickly he was moving to complete Jesus' burial before the Sabbath), and the law states that any Jewish person who comes into contact with a dead body is considered unclean for seven days (see Num. 19:11–14).

Despite that, Joseph continued on, and Pilate ordered that Jesus' body be given to him (see Matt. 27:58). As it was getting later and time was not on his side, Joseph found an accomplice—Nicodemus (see John 19:39).

Nicodemus was also on the Jewish council with Joseph and had personally met Jesus at one point. Nicodemus had visited Jesus at night, in secret (see 3:1–21), probably for the same reason that Joseph had been following Jesus in secret—fear of the Jewish leaders. Nicodemus had a conversation with Jesus about eternal life and being born again, and an interesting part of that exchange is that Nicodemus used the plural "we" several times.

No one other than Jesus and Nicodemus is quoted as speaking in that conversation, so we can't say for sure whether someone else was with Nicodemus, but there is more than enough evidence to indicate that others on the council of the Sanhedrin may have been there and held similar beliefs to those of Nicodemus. The other council members were almost certainly aware of Nicodemus going to meet Jesus, and Nicodemus probably reported back to them. One of them could have been Joseph of Arimathea, and Nicodemus' retelling of his encounter with Jesus could have been the thing that solidified Joseph's belief in Jesus. So it is not entirely surprising that Nicodemus aided Joseph in the burial of Jesus.

Joseph saying "yes" to his rich-young-ruler moment posed a rich-young-ruler moment for Nicodemus as well. Nicodemus didn't just agree to show up at the scene of Jesus' death—he also hauled with him a seventy-five-pound mixture of myrrh and aloe to put on Jesus' body (see John 19:39–40). I don't know the last time you hauled seventy-five pounds of anything, but as I've discovered doing CrossFit, it's no small task.

By now evening was upon them, and nightfall was just around the corner. They didn't have time to take Jesus' freshly prepared body just anywhere, and they didn't want to advertise all over town what they were doing. They needed somewhere close. So Joseph decided to take Jesus' body to a tomb that he knew was close by and ready to go, because it was his tomb (see Matt. 27:60). His actions inadvertently fulfilled a prophesy found in Isaiah 53:9: "He was assigned a grave with the wicked, and with the rich in his death, though he had done no violence, nor was any deceit in his mouth." This was just one of many prophesies confirming that Jesus was in fact the Son of God and the true Messiah.

Relieved to finish before the Sabbath, Joseph rolled a large stone (more like a boulder) in front of the entrance of the tomb and left (see Matt. 27:60). While the burial story ends here and we never hear about Joseph of Arimathea again, we know that Joseph's role in the burial of Jesus did not stay a secret for long.

The chief priests were well aware of Joseph going to Pilate behind their backs, because they went to Pilate and asked for the tomb to be made secure in their concern that the disciples would try to steal and hide Jesus' body (see 27:62–66).

Here we are with two very similar men: Joseph of Arimathea and the rich young ruler. Both were men of wealth and influence, both desired to inherit eternal life, both were faced with a decision that had to be made in an instant, and both had a lot riding on that moment.

But only one man made the decision to use his wealth and influence to properly care for the only One in all of history to defeat death. Only one man was privileged to see, touch and carry the body of the Son of God.

Only one man risked nearly everything because following Jesus (even after His death) was more important to him than his position, wealth or reputation. Only one man gave up his own tomb, knowing that in doing so he could no longer keep his belief in Jesus a secret (even though Jesus wouldn't need his tomb for long).

These two men could have had such similar stories, so why didn't they? Because Joseph of Arimathea never viewed his wealth and influence as his. It was never about him—it was always about Jesus. From the very first decision to go to Pilate to the last roll of the stone against the tomb, Joseph thought only about how he could serve Jesus, and that kind of thinking allowed him to be part of the most miraculous story ever told.

The rich young ruler, on the other hand, could never get past himself. All he could think about was what giving up his wealth would mean for him, and that inward focus caused him to miss out on following Jesus during His physical time on earth. Two stories, two decisions, two very different outcomes.

The Rich-Young-Ruler Moment of Zacchaeus

Maybe it is because I was a youth pastor for thirteen years, or maybe it's because I am a mother to four children under the age of nine, but every time I hear Zacchaeus' name, all I can think about are the lyrics to this kids' song:

> Zacchaeus was a wee little man,
> And a wee little man was he.
> He climbed up in a sycamore tree,
> For the Lord he wanted to see.
> And as the Savior passed that way,
> He looked up in the tree,
> And he said, "Zacchaeus, you come down,
> For I'm going to your house today.
> For I'm going to your house today."[2]

Because of this song, I never gave much thought to Zacchaeus beside the facts that he was short, he climbed a tree to see Jesus, and Jesus had gone to his house. Oddly comical, but not really exciting.

But when I started looking more closely at Zacchaeus, I was truly inspired by his heart change, especially in light of the rich young ruler's story. The differences in the two responses were astounding.

Zacchaeus was a chief tax collector, and he was intensely hated by the Jewish people. This kind of animosity toward tax collectors is still felt somewhat today—I mean, no one is particularly excited about having to deal with the Internal Revenue Service—but we don't in any way have the same level of hatred toward them that the people of Jericho possessed toward Zacchaeus.

In the New Testament, the position of tax collector was one that people bid on. It wasn't like an election; the people doing the bidding were the people who wanted the position, like at an auction. So what did they bid?

Well, they bid a certain amount of money that they would raise for the government through collecting taxes, and the person who bid the highest amount would win the job. Basically, whoever committed to stealing the most money from the Jewish people won the bid. The tax collector got to keep any money brought in over and above the committed amount.

The chief tax collector received a double bonus, because he oversaw all the tax collectors in his region; so he not only made money off the taxes, he also received a percentage of what was collected by each of the other tax collectors. If we imagine a corrupt pyramid scheme and then pretend that it has no regulations on it whatsoever, we will start to get an idea of the reputation tax collectors had in their cities.

Jericho was a particularly lucrative city for a chief tax collector because it was the center for the export of balsam (better known today as turpentine), which was used in costly substances such as frankincense and myrrh. Many travelers, merchants and soldiers used the road that ran through Jericho to Jerusalem, so all of this activity produced quite a bit of tax revenue for the tax collectors.

For Zacchaeus to have won the bid and kept it, he must have extorted a lot of money from the people of Jericho and put pressure on his staff to do the same.

Here's the real kicker: the people he was harassing for money never saw much benefit from their tax payments, because portions of it went to the Roman Empire and the rest to the tax collectors. Despite the fact that Zacchaeus' name literally means "pure one," he was the worst kind of cheat.

Unlike the stories of the rich young ruler and Joseph of Arimathea, the entire action between Jesus and Zacchaeus is told only in the Gospel of Luke.

> Jesus entered Jericho and was passing through. A man was there by the name of Zacchaeus; he was a chief tax collector and was wealthy. He wanted to see who Jesus was, but because he was short he could not see over the crowd. So he ran ahead and climbed a sycamore-fig tree to see him, since Jesus was coming that way.
>
> When Jesus reached the spot, he looked up and said to him, "Zacchaeus, come down immediately. I must stay at your house today." So he came down at once and welcomed him gladly.
>
> All the people saw this and began to mutter, "He has gone to be the guest of a sinner."

> But Zacchaeus stood up and said to the Lord, "Look, Lord! Here and now I give half of my possessions to the poor, and if I have cheated anybody out of anything, I will pay back four times the amount."
>
> Jesus said to him, "Today salvation has come to this house, because this man, too, is a son of Abraham. For the Son of Man came to seek and to save the lost." (Luke 19:1–10)

As we have seen, Jericho was a city that many travelers passed through on their way to Jerusalem, and that is exactly what Jesus and His disciples were doing when this exchange between Zacchaeus and Jesus took place.

Zacchaeus was short in stature. What was the average height of an Israelite during the time of the judges (from the fourteenth to the eleventh century BC)? The roof height of excavated houses of that period suggests that the typical Israelite was only about five feet tall.[3] So for Zacchaeus to be described as short in this text, he was probably significantly shorter than five feet.

Zacchaeus' physical build might have been a constant source of embarrassment and ridicule for him when he was growing up, which could have led to his ability to steal from people and cheat them with no sense of remorse. But then came Jesus; and from that moment on, Zacchaeus had a series of rich-young-ruler moments.

Picture it. Zacchaeus had gotten word that Jesus was coming through town; and the stories of His miracles, His challenges toward Jewish leaders, and His claim to be the Son of God had preceded Him. Zacchaeus wanted to see Jesus; but as the crowd formed around him, he knew that he was too short to see and would miss his one chance. He knew the city well—he had walked the streets thousands of times collecting taxes—and he knew of a sycamore tree along Jesus' route (sycamore trees are great climbing trees). He thought that if he ran ahead of the crowd and climbed the tree, he would be able to see Jesus.

Rich-young-ruler moment number one: If Zacchaeus acted on his idea, he would bring even more ridicule on himself, because climbing a tree would make quite the spectacle to the crowd—but he did it anyway. His desire to see Jesus outweighed any sense of self-dignity.

Zacchaeus waited in the tree; and as Jesus walked by with the crowd following Him, He stopped and looked directly up at Zacchaeus and called him by name.

This must have taken Zacchaeus by surprise. He hadn't been trying to talk to Jesus; he just wanted to see Him. He never even intended to be seen by Jesus, much less acknowledged by name. If truth be told, this was probably one of the rare times Zacchaeus heard his name in a positive light.

I love how, despite the chaos and noise, Jesus called Zacchaeus by name. It shows how personal Jesus is and that He is never too busy to speak hope and life into someone, even if just by a mention of that person's name. And Jesus did not stop there—He asked to stay at Zacchaeus' house.

Zacchaeus probably had a million questions running through his mind at that moment. How did Jesus know his name? Why did He want to stay at his house? Didn't Jesus know what kind of man he was?

Someone like Jesus didn't talk to someone like Zacchaeus, much less come to his house. There were many more honorable men who would gladly have allowed Him to stay at their house. But only one question had to be answered: Would Zacchaeus get out of the tree?

Rich-young-ruler moment number two: Zacchaeus did climb down—and not gradually with a cautious spirit, but rather, as the Scripture says, "he came down at once and welcomed [Jesus] gladly" (Luke 19:6).

Maybe it was as Zacchaeus made his way down to Jesus or as he stood in front of Him, but Zacchaeus began to hear the "mutters" of the people, and he knew that Jesus could hear them too. Then one of the most radical surrenders of obedience recorded in the Bible took place.

Rich-young-ruler moment number three: Standing in the presence of Jesus and simultaneously hearing his reputation as a sinner spoken in front of a holy God, Zacchaeus was moved to repentance and said, "Look, Lord! Here and now I give half of my possessions to the poor, and if I have cheated anybody out of anything, I will pay back four times the amount" (19:8).

Wow! What a stark contrast to the rich young ruler! Two wealthy men, both in the presence of Jesus, but one was so moved by Jesus that he voluntarily—in fact, he came up with the idea himself—gave away half of his possessions to the poor. But Zacchaeus went even further. He didn't want to just *appear* generous. He wanted to right his wrongs—to go above and beyond in his repentance.

I'm not sure why Zacchaeus said "*if* I have cheated anybody out of anything," because he knew that he had, and Jesus knew it too. Maybe he wanted to try and salvage some sort of credibility.

Regardless, Zacchaeus committed to give away four times the amount that he had poached from people—far beyond paying back what he had stolen. By coming down from the tree and welcoming Jesus gladly, Zacchaeus had already offered himself; but by giving away his wealth, he offered his heart and priorities to Jesus. He offered all he had. Zacchaeus had finally lived up to the true meaning of his name—"pure one." "Blessed are the *pure* in heart, for they will see God" (Matt. 5:8).

Jesus responded to Zacchaeus' offering, "Today salvation has come to this house, because this man, too, is a son of Abraham. For the Son of Man came to seek and to save the lost" (Luke 19:9–10).

It had been quite a while since Zacchaeus had been considered Jewish, because no good Jew would have been a tax collector, much less a chief tax collector. Jesus publicly redefined Zacchaeus' identify from sinner to saved, while reminding everyone that he was in fact a son of Abraham.

Jesus was also sure to address everyone's concern about His intermingling with sinners by clarifying that His sole purpose in becoming the Son of Man was "to seek and to save the lost."

The story of Zacchaeus is a story of pure salvation. It is a visual illustration of what Jesus was talking about when He had responded to the rich young ruler who walked away sad: "Children, how hard it is to enter the kingdom of God! It is easier for a camel to go through the eye of a needle than for someone who is rich to enter the kingdom of God. . . . With man this is impossible, but not with God; all things are possible with God" (Mark 10:24–27).

When we look at the rich young ruler and Zacchaeus, the odds are in favor of the rich young ruler following Jesus. Think about it. If I came up to you and said, "Two men love money and have a lot of it. One has followed the commandments his entire life and desperately desires to know how to inherit eternal life. The other has built his fortune on stealing and taking advantage of other people; he followed Jewish custom as a boy but has not been faithful to God for years. Which one is more likely to answer Jesus' call to follow Him?" You would probably choose the first man all day long!

Sure, the rich young man followed the rules with his actions; but he was unwilling to surrender his most prized possession, his wealth. On his own, it was impossible for him to inherit eternal life. It was also impossible for Zacchaeus to inherit eternal life on his own; but when Jesus saw that he was willing to surrender everything, the impossible became possible with God.

Clement of Alexandria

We don't hear any more about Zacchaeus after the book of Luke. But Clement of Alexandria (also known as Titus Flavius Clemens), a well-known theologian from the end of the first century to the first part of the second century, introduces an interesting theory about Zacchaeus.

In his writings in the *Stromata*, Clement claims that Zacchaeus' name was later changed to Matthias by the apostles: "Zacchaeus whom they call Matthias, the chief tax collector, when he had heard that the Lord had esteemed him highly enough to be with him, said, 'Behold, half of my present possessions I give as alms, and Lord, if I ever extorted money from anyone in any way, I return it fourfold.'"[4] Then, in Acts 1:21–26, we find out that Matthias took the place of Judas as a disciple after Jesus' ascension.

> Therefore it is necessary to choose one of the men who have been with us the whole time the Lord Jesus was living among us, beginning from John's baptism to the time when Jesus was taken up from us. For one of these must become a witness with us of his resurrection."

> So they nominated two men: Joseph called Barsabbas (also known as Justus) and Matthias. Then they prayed, "Lord, you know everyone's heart. Show us which of these two you have chosen to take over this apostolic ministry, which Judas left to go where he belongs." Then they cast lots, and the lot fell to Matthias; so he was added to the eleven apostles. (Acts 1:21–26)

A debate exists in the theological world as to whether Clement's theory is true, mainly because Acts 1:21–22 says, "It is necessary to choose one of the men who have been with us the whole time the Lord Jesus was living among us, beginning from John's baptism to the time when Jesus was taken up from us," and Zacchaeus was likely not with Jesus from the time He was baptized by John the Baptist.

However, Clement's theory should not be pushed aside, because at the time that Clement was in Alexandria writing the *Stromata*, the city was known as a beacon for learning and information, which started with the Library of Alexandria. The library was part of a larger research institution called the Museum of Alexandria, where many of the most famous thinkers of the ancient world studied.

So, though we don't know if Clement's theory is true, we do know that he had access to the best collection of historical documentation of his time. It is possible that Clement had access to documentation showing that Matthias and Zacchaeus were the same person, documentation that we simply don't have access to now. Unfortunately, most of those documents were destroyed with the destruction of the Library of Alexandria in the seventh century.[5] Another point to keep in mind is that Clement writes as if his premise is a well-known fact, not something he is uncovering for the first time. If Clement's statement about Zacchaeus is true, what a beautiful story of redemption it displays (not that it doesn't already).

We see a man who went from having the worst reputation of a sinner—someone truly hated by all—to being part of Jesus' inner circle. It would have been impossible for Zacchaeus to know, at the moment he was sitting in a sycamore tree, what the future held for him. It would have been impossible for him to know what his "yes" would produce, just as it is impossible for us know what our "yes" could produce.

Saying "yes," as we have seen, isn't just about the blessings we experience here in the present, but also about the blessings we gain eternally. Whether or not Zacchaeus went on to be one of the Twelve, his purity of heart allowed him to see God both in the present and eternally.

The bottom line is this: what we give up for God can never compare to what He offers us in return. For Zacchaeus that was a new identity—worth much more than half of his possessions.

Never the Same

The thing I love about both Joseph of Arimathea and Zacchaeus is that they said "yes" to glorifying God in their everyday lives with their everyday occupations. They were not priests; they were not Jesus' disciples; they were just ordinary men willing to make extraordinary sacrifices.

The decisions we make in our defining moments will either lead us toward God or away from Him. The decision of the rich young ruler led him away from God. But Joseph of Arimathea and Zacchaeus were never the same as they launched into new lives of reflecting Christ.

I wish we could continue to follow the lives of Joseph and Zacchaeus, because I am certain that this was not the last time these two men were faced with rich-young-ruler moments. The rest of their lives must have been full of them.

This has been true for me—and it's been true for many others whose lives I have been privileged to watch as they have tirelessly pursued the Lord.

8

I'm Just Ordinary—What Can I Do for God?

I have a genuine fear of failure. I'm also claustrophobic and afraid of the dark. (That has nothing to do with failure—I'm just trying to set up a safe place so that you'll feel comfortable with getting real about your own uncertainties.) Basically, I have the same fears as your average seven-year-old. Actually, all of my fears can probably be traced back to when I was seven.

When I was young, my two older brothers loved to sit on me, and they wouldn't get up until I cried. Or they would hold me over our banister by my ankles; and if I had moved, I would have fallen to my death. (They are delightful; I would love for you to meet them one day.)

My fear of failure runs deep, to the point that most of my life decisions have not revolved around what would bring Jesus the most glory, but around whether I would be good at something. If I didn't think I would succeed at something, I just didn't do it. But what's crazy is that I am not the only one who struggles with this.

Fear is a culprit that holds many amazingly gifted people back from true greatness. The tricky thing about fear is that it is not always a terrifying experience that leaves us feeling as if we had just watched a horror movie; sometimes fear is much more understated.

It can simply mean thinking less of ourselves than we should, so that we never have the courage to try something daring. It can be a voice that whispers in our ears all the things we *aren't* rather than everything we *are*. The reason I so desperately latched on to my checklist of life is because it made me feel safe, secure and successful.

For the first twenty-eight years of my life, every time I felt a nudge toward something outside my realm of safety into the unknown possibility of failure, my response to God was always something like, "I'm *just* a __________; I can't __________."

- "I'm just a teenager; I can't lead a Bible study with adults in it."
- "I'm just an ordinary woman; I can't teach Your Word."
- "I'm just an associate level staff member; I can't stand up to leadership."

This quickly turned into something more along the lines of, "I'm *not* ______________; I can't ______________."

- "I'm not as talented as Jen Hatmaker; I can't write a book."
- "I'm not a stay-at-home mom; we can't adopt."
- "I'm not wealthy enough; I can't give to that need."
- "I'm not qualified enough for that job; I can't apply."

God's List

We all have lists of fears that too often drive the direction of our life. But the great news is that God has a list on us too. Here is part of it:

- We are "fearfully and wonderfully made" (Ps. 139:14).
- We are a "new creation. . . . The old has gone!" (2 Cor. 5:17).
- We were not given a spirit of timidity, but one of "power, love and self-discipline" (2 Tim. 1:7).
- We were created in God's image (see Gen. 1:27).
- We have been crowned "with love and compassion" (Ps. 103:4).

And you know what? None of the items on God's list say that we have to be anything more than the most surrendered version of ourselves. They don't say that we have go to Africa or start a nonprofit organization. We don't have to become a pastor or start a Christian compound. (In fact, I would really discourage you from that last one—that's crossing over into the too-odd-for-God category.)

There is no one right way to do this thing that we call Christianity. If there were, then we would all have the exact same stories, and Christianity really *would* be boring. God is a creative God, and He shows off His creativity in His creation.

When we try to be someone other than who God created us to be or don't trust Him to give us all we need, we stifle the creativity of the God who literally spoke the entire solar system into existence. Fear is actually pretty insulting to God, if we think about it. When the Lord is leading us to act on something, it is because He already knows that we have what it takes! He has already empowered us with the perfect skill set for the job, and that is why He asks *us*—not the person we are convinced is more talented or just flat-out better. If He weren't convinced that we were the perfect person for the job, He would have asked someone else.

Saying "Yes" to God—in Our Ordinary Lives

Whenever I talk to people about how my life has radically changed, I am always asked some form of these two questions:

1. I want to do what God is asking me to do, but how do I know what He is asking?
2. I don't even know where to start. How did you start?

When I hear these questions, I am reminded of Paul's straightforward words in Romans.

> By the grace given me I say to every one of you: Do not think of yourself more highly than you ought, but rather think of yourself with sober judgment, in accordance with the faith God has distributed to each of you. For just as each of us has one body with many members, and these members do not all have the same function, so in Christ we, though many, form one body, and each member belongs to all the others. We have different gifts, according to the grace given to each of us. If your gift is prophesying, then prophesy in accordance with your faith; if it is serving, then serve; if it is teaching, then teach; if it is to encourage, then give encouragement; if it is giving, then give generously; if it is to lead, do it diligently; if it is to show mercy, do it cheerfully. (12:3–8)

Paul was saying, "Open your eyes and look around for the people you can help by using the natural gifts you already have." God is not mystical or confusing; we are the ones determined to make things complicated. God has only one desire and that is to bring glory to Himself. Who do you think He uses to bring Himself that glory? That's right, His children!

It is of no benefit to God for His children to be confused. There is a reason that we live on the street we do, in the neighborhood we do, in the city we do. There is a reason we work at the company we do, in the cubicle next to the person we do.

If God has not moved us yet, it is because He is not done using us to bring Him glory right where we are. I wasted too much time waiting for the booming voice or the writing in the sky.

Stop thinking about everything you aren't, and start living in the fullness of who God made you to be. Start working right where you are, and be on the lookout for every rich-young-ruler moment that comes your way. God will take it from there.

Maybe you're thinking, *This is a really powerful message; but I work in a cubicle from nine to five, so what does living a truly blessed life look like for me?* or, *Redefining the word "blessed" sounds amazing, but I'm so exhausted and covered in spit-up that I can't even think straight*. And you're in good company.

Before I started writing this chapter, I cleaned my kitchen, which smelled as if something had died in my sink. Tomorrow when I wake up, four grumpy little people will want to eat breakfast, put on clean clothes and have a lunch packed, so they don't have to eat the school cafeteria burrito. (Good grief, they are so high maintenance with wanting to eat and be clean *all the time.*)

Nothing I do in that 6:00 a.m. to 7:15 a.m. time frame makes me feel much like I am advancing the kingdom of God. But in that hour and fifteen minutes, the way I love and serve those kids will paint a picture to them of the unconditional love that Jesus has for them and how they are to love others.

I don't know anyone who has the luxury of sitting around and reading the Bible all day. And if anyone does have that kind of time, sitting around and constantly reading is not what God would want us to do—that's not what Jesus did, anyway.

He used ordinary people with ordinary professions to do extraordinary things. He used situations from everyday life to teach unshakable truths, because that is what people could understand.

Over the years, I have gotten to know some people whose lives appear rather mundane but are anything but normal. They are just ordinary people, but these men and women decided to say "yes" to the rich-young-ruler moments that came their way and intentionally pursue lives defined only by Jesus' grace.

I am honored to say that these people are my friends, and each of them inspires me constantly to live authentically and not to be defined by the standards of society but by God's standard.

I want to introduce several of my friends to you in the hope that you will be as inspired by their stories as I have been. Each one is a true picture of a blessed life.

Blessed Are Those Who Mourn

When you meet Cathy Crossno for the first time, you either instantly have a friend crush on her, or you are so jealous of her that you can hardly stand it. She is kind, thoughtful, beautiful, a great wife and mother, and in no way looks as if she has had five babies! She wants to be great at everything she does, and for the most part she is nailing it!

I met Cathy and her husband, James, at church. I wanted to get to know her better; but she had two kids and soon added two more, and I had three kids and was in the process of adopting our fourth.

Consequently, she and I never got around to seeing each other outside the passing, "Hi, how are you?" between church services. Little did I know that the Lord was about to orchestrate a deep bond between Cathy and I.

One day my office phone rang.

"Hey, Jenny, it's Cathy Crossno. Can I come to your office? I need to talk to you."

"Uh, sure. Let me know when you want to schedule something."

"I can come right now. I can be there in a few minutes."

I honestly thought that Cathy was coming to complain about something at our church, particularly our kids' ministry. Not because Cathy is like that—she is pretty much the opposite—but in my job no news was good news; so normally when a parent wanted to meet, it was because something wasn't going well.

About fifteen minutes later, Cathy showed up at my office. Never in my wildest dreams could I have imagined the story that was about to unfold.

Cathy grew up in a devoutly Catholic family in Amarillo, Texas. She is incredibly thankful for her Catholic upbringing, because it built within her a desire to respect the boundaries in Christianity. But she never knew about the relational side of Jesus, and because of that Cathy was a rule follower.

She didn't drink until she was twenty-one, never did drugs, and decided in high school (despite significant pressure from her boyfriend) that her virginity was precious and she was going to try and wait until marriage to have sex. She was a cheerleader, popular and very much your all-American-type girl.

After attending junior college for a couple of years, Cathy headed to Denton, Texas to attend the University of North Texas. She started dating an older guy, but she soon realized that the relationship was not a healthy one and that she needed to end it. Unfortunately, breaking up was not as cut-and-dried as Cathy had wanted.

In the process of ending things, she found out she was pregnant. It wasn't the result of a night of passion or love, but a night of foolish decisions gone too far.

As soon as Cathy found out she was pregnant, she knew that the Lord wanted her to put the baby up for adoption. She'd had no experience whatsoever with adoption. She didn't know anyone who was adopted or had adopted. But it was a leading from the Lord she could not ignore.

At the end of her fall semester, Cathy returned to Amarillo to be close to family for the remainder of her pregnancy. Though her family was incredibly supportive, they were not in total alignment with Cathy's choice to give the baby up for adoption—they tried to convince her to raise the baby at home with their help.

But the Lord gave Cathy the strength to stay the course of adoption. (This was not in any way an easy decision for her. The day she sat in my office and told this story, tears streamed down her face. Cathy was not saying "yes" to adoption—she was saying "yes" to the Lord. Sometimes rich-young-ruler moments aren't thrilling and adventurous; sometimes they are heartbreaking and beautiful all at the same time.) One day, during the winter, Cathy went for a seemingly routine haircut. She'd had her hair cut by a woman named Debra her entire life and had formed a close relationship with her over the years. While still at school, Cathy had heard that Debra had struggled with getting pregnant, had miscarried a baby and had lost twins at birth the previous July.

As she reconnected with Debra that day, Cathy began to feel that she wanted Debra and her husband, Steve, to adopt her baby. By the time she got home after her haircut, she was certain. Cathy had no idea if they were even interested in adoption; but later that week she and her mother went to Debra and Steve's house, and Cathy told them her entire story. Then, in a vulnerable and risky move, she revealed to them that she knew of their fertility issues and felt that they were supposed to adopt her baby.

Debra told her that she had felt the very same thing the moment she had heard that Cathy was pregnant and had elected adoption. So that day Debra and Steve accepted the greatest gift anyone can give to another person—the gift of life. But that's not the end of the story. Nope, God was just getting started.

Being faithful to obey God is not always just a one-time commitment; sometimes we have to say "yes" over and over, and it gets harder and harder. Well, the time came for Cathy, Debra and Steve to find out the gender of the baby.

When the ultrasound was finished, and Debra and Steve were congratulated on their new daughter, Cathy felt that their celebration was her sorrow—for the first of many times. Cathy knew that this was only the beginning of a tough road ahead for her.

That's when Cathy decided to find a support group. Fifteen years ago adoption was not as prevalent, or even as accepted, as it is today, but Cathy found her way into a grief-recovery group for parents who had lost a child—and in a sense she was going to lose a child.

It took a while for the people in the group to accept Cathy, because every week, as she grew larger with child, it was a harsh reality to them that Cathy was willfully giving up what they could never get back. Being pregnant gave Cathy a sort of scarlet letter; living in the grace of Jesus Christ was extremely difficult for her during this time.

Lexi was born on July 3, 2001, and Cathy describes the three days she spent in the hospital with Lexi as the best three days of her life. She remembers looking down at Lexi and wondering, *Will this baby ever know how much I love her and that I am doing what I feel God wants for her?*

Cathy and Lexi were showered with love and support, and Cathy's mom video-recorded nearly the entire three days. They even had a priest come to the hospital to baptize Lexi and read a blessing over her life. Cathy's mom bought two stuffed-animal pigs—one stayed next to Lexi in her bassinet, and one stayed with Cathy in her hospital bed. On day three, when the nurses came to take Lexi, Cathy and Lexi traded stuffed pigs, and to this day Cathy sleeps with that pig every single night.

Cathy simply said, "The day Lexi left my hospital room, a part of me went with her." Mothers who give up their babies might be the bravest, most selfless people in the world.

On her way home from the hospital, Cathy stopped to have her photos of Lexi developed. She surrounded herself with pictures of Lexi to make sure that she would never forgot her.

Debra and Steve were incredibly gracious and allowed Cathy to be involved in Lexi's life as much or as little as she wanted, but Cathy headed back to university a month after Lexi was born.

Debra and Steve occasionally sent pictures and letters to Cathy, which made checking the mail the highlight of her day. This pattern allowed Cathy to be a part of Lexi's life, but also allowed everyone to settle into their new normal.

Cathy spent the next summer at home in Amarillo. The day she was leaving to head back to school, she stopped to run one last errand. As Cathy pulled up to the Pack 'n' Mail, almost one year to the day after Lexi was born, she looked over to see Debra's car parked right next to hers—and Lexi in the backseat.

Debra soon noticed Cathy, and they got out of their cars and hugged each other. Debra asked Cathy if she wanted to see Lexi, and for the first time since she had left her hospital room, Cathy laid eyes on Lexi. As mom to an adopted child, I have many times imagined what it would be like to meet my daughter's birth mother—what I would say, how I would handle myself, what I would want her to know about the little girl to whom we are both mom.

My daughter's story is very different from Lexi's, but one thing is similar: both Cathy and my daughter's birth mother did the same thing I would have done if I had been unable to give my child the best life possible; they found a way.

Sure, situations of abuse exist where Child Protective Services needs to intervene, but most birth mothers who choose adoption are just like Cathy and voluntarily decide to do something beyond comprehension in order to show a love beyond comprehension. Doesn't that sound familiar? God deliberately sent His Son for us to show a love that is beyond comprehension.

A relationship began between Lexi and Cathy and their families that day. They started to celebrate holidays together. In fact, when Cathy married James, guess who her flower girl and matron of honor were? Yep, Lexi and Debra. Lexi is now fourteen and has never experienced an absence of relationship with her birth mother. Having a relationship with Lexi has been a precious gift, but Cathy has still faced bumps in the road. Lexi struggled with questions related to her adoption as she witnessed Cathy's now-happy family of four kids. Lexi never witnessed the season of Cathy's life when she was single and pregnant; all Lexi has known is the more-than-capable parenting she sees in James and Cathy now.

These questions are hard and sometimes unanswerable. But Cathy has the rare gift of being able to influence her biological child and watch her grow up, and Lexi gets the almost unheard of gift of direct communication with her birth mother. Though the relationship is not always easy and, at times, is really messy, it is blessed.

Cathy had not come into my office that day to complain. She had come in to share her deeply personal story with me because she wanted to offer support to our family in our own adoption process, from her unique perspective as a birth mother—particularly as Kennedy grew older and started asking Chad and me questions about her biological family. Cathy had come in abruptly because she wanted to seize the moment while she was still brave enough to tell me. How precious is that?

As Cathy finished telling me her story, I asked her, "What would you want people to know about saying 'yes' to such a hard leading from the Lord?"

She answered, "People need to realize that just because someone is making decisions that look different from theirs, that person is still struggling with those decisions, and they need grace and prayer.

God doesn't give us the strength to get through the hard stuff until we need it. I truly believe that because I followed His will, He blessed me with James, our four kids and a relationship with Lexi."

Lexi with her birth mother, Cathy

Blessed Are Those Who Hunger and Thirst for Righteousness

I met Kristian Rose when I was smack dab in the middle of my spiritual crisis. Kristian was instrumental in my choice to wrestle with my faith, mainly because I couldn't get through even one conversation with him without being challenged to rethink the entire way I lived . . . not to mention that the guy is just flat-out smart—like sickening smart. He reads law journals and John Piper just for fun. He's an oddly fascinating person.

I met Kristian at Love146, the organization I wrote about in chapter 3 that works to end child sex trafficking. When I was floundering in my faith and desperately trying to live out a life that reflected Jesus' teachings, I started reaching out to organizations that I was passionate about to see if I could offer them my services.

Fighting child trafficking was most important to me, but I am not a special ops agent—I can't perform a raid on a brothel and I am not a social worker, so I felt pretty limited in what I could do. But as Paul said in Romans 12, we all have different gifts, so I contacted the Love146 Houston office and asked if I could do any administrative work to help out. I started showing up every week on my day off. I didn't do anything revolutionary—I mostly wrote thank-you letters to donors, entered data into the computer, made information packets and checked the mail. But my time in that office affected my heart, and watching and talking to Kristian was a huge part of that.

I have never known a couple who live out their convictions as deeply as Kristian and his wife, Katy. If I ever have a moment of thinking, *You know, we're really nailing it right now*, I can call Kristian and quickly realize how far my family has to go in living out a missional calling.

For example, Kristian and Katy have rice-and-beans night every Monday in order to give a literal picture to their three young sons of how the majority of the world lives. When I told Kristian how great an idea that was, he responded, "Well, we don't just do it to show them how the rest of the world eats. We also want to arrange our budget so that we are required to eat like the rest of the world."

I love this family and the way they intentionally fight to live out the gospel and love those around them in every part of their lives—even at dinnertime.

Kristian and Katy grew up in a wealthy suburb outside Dallas. As Kristian told me, "The American dream was not only normal in our surroundings, but you were almost looked down on if you didn't pursue it." Kristian and Katy's first date was to their senior prom, which is totally adorable. They dated throughout college and spent a lot of time talking about their priorities and what was important for them to pursue.

As they developed in their faith, they became exposed to many injustices—not only globally but also in the United States—and they wanted to devote their lives to helping end these atrocities. Katy wanted to work for a nonprofit organization. Kristian considered becoming a pastor; but he also struggled with how the American church seemed so inwardly focused, and he went through a time of not wanting anything to do with the local church.

I was in that place two years ago and actually became so disenchanted with the church and my Christian checklists that I tried to get out of the ministry altogether. But every time I tried to leave, the door was consistently shut. God didn't want me to give up on the local church, and He didn't want Kristian to quit either.

But it is hard not to feel angry about building campaigns and million-dollar facilities with bowling alleys and indoor swimming pools when vulnerable kids are being trafficked due to poverty or abandonment.

Katy and Kristian eventually ended up moving to East Harlem in New York City, because at that time New York was one of only three cities offering survivor care for those who were victims of trafficking, an issue about which they were both passionate. Katy got a job offer at a domestic violence prevention organization; and Kristian, believe it or not, went on staff at a church as the pastor of community and justice (which is basically an Avenger-type way of saying that he was the missions pastor).

Take a look at a few statistics on East Harlem.

- The neighborhood suffers from many social issues, such as the highest unemployment rate in New York City, teenage pregnancy, AIDS, drug abuse homelessness, and an asthma rate five times the national average.
- It has the second highest concentration of public housing in the United States, closely following Brownsville, Brooklyn.[1]
- The percent of residents living below the poverty level is nearly twice as high as in Manhattan and NYC overall.
- 21 percent of the population do not have more than an eighth grade education.[2]

Moving from a suburb of Dallas to East Harlem constitutes what I like to call culture shock. But Kristian and Katy had a ton of exposure to the impoverished, exploited and abused, and in that process they met many amazing people who were running soup kitchens out of their basements and transporting food and hygiene products to the homeless community in the backs of vans.

The people in New York who made the biggest differences were not the well-known Christian leaders and pastors but, rather, volunteers who will probably never be known or recognized. While these people were making a difference, they were merely scratching the surface of a much larger issue.

Kristian's position at the church enabled him to interact with many groups (including Love146), tirelessly working to address the biggest needs in East Harlem; and as he watched them, he realized that the only real difference between a good idea and one that changes the world is a good strategy. If Kristian is anything, he is a strategist.

So Katy and Kristian made another bold decision—Kristian decided to apply to law school with the hopes of not just making a dent in these injustices, but helping to end them. Though they loved living in the city, with Kristian going back to school and their first child on the way, this was not feasible.

So the Rose family went through another season of culture shock, this time by leaving East Harlem and moving to Norman, Oklahoma, where Kristian attended law school at the University of Oklahoma.

As the end of law school approached, Kristian expected to get a job at a law firm, pay off student-loan debt, possibly volunteer for some nongovernment organizations (maybe even serve on a board or two) and, as he puts it, "not just be a doer but a funder as well; there are a lot of doers but not many funders."

Around this time Kristian was contacted by Love146 to see if he was interested in applying for a new position they were creating—the Texas director of operations and general counsel. This is where the rubber met the road for the Rose family.

For most of us, moving to East Harlem or applying to law school or becoming foster parents (which Kristian and Katy later did) would have been really difficult decisions, but Kristian talks about all of these as if they were normal decisions that anyone would have easily made.

But when he talks about deciding whether or not to work for Love146, he describes it as extremely difficult and emotional. He was in such distress about the decision that he actually broke down emotionally while talking to his father about it one night. This was the Rose family's rich-young-ruler moment. Kristian had just spent four years in school. Throughout that time, he had worked only during breaks to support his family which now consisted of two small children and, because of a new desire to become foster parents, was going to expand.

He also had student-loan debt. And while Love146 is a great organization to support because every dollar they receive is stretched to its limits, it also means that their staff has to maintain lean lifestyles.

Kristian and Katy Rose

Kristian and Katy were passionate about the issue of trafficking; but they also had to feed, clothe and provide shelter for their children, and the math didn't add up—they didn't know how they could say "yes." To Kristian, the decision felt like choosing between his dream job and providing for his family.

Despite his fear and anxiety, Kristian chose to say "yes" to God, and he accepted the job. The exploited and abused kids in the Houston area who are now being rescued and cared for through the amazing work that Kristian and his team do at Love146 are surely grateful. And while Houston may not be East Harlem, the Rose family is still finding ways to live "missionally." Katy has been active in ministering to, and living life alongside, many displaced refugee families. And Kristian has had many opportunities to teach about missional living in local churches all over the area. Most recently, they welcomed the adoption of a son. Four states, three kids and many jobs later, they are blessed.

Blessed Are the Merciful

Jackie Hooks is unlike anyone I have ever known. She is captivating and extroverted, and she makes everyone she meets feel loved and important. Some people might initially find her a little overwhelming, because she has such a big personality; but she is so incredibly friendly that she wins people over and probably has them serving food to the homeless or providing diapers to teenage moms. No lie—she is that influential.

Jackie is a connector. She builds bridges between those who don't have and those who do; she is the best ever at bringing people together. And if she is not talking *about* Jesus, she is talking *to* Him. Yes, she literally talks to Jesus—like all the time—and He talks back, and she listens. She loves Jesus with her whole being, and she is willing to do just about anything to get others to love Him too.

Jackie lives here in the Houston area, and it is hard to find someone in my community who does not know her in some way. For example, in a one-week period the following things happened. While at my daughter's swim meet, I volunteered to be a timer. Every lane needs two timers, and typically we are paired with a complete stranger. The stranger I was paired with knew Jackie. A few days later I took my kids to the movies. The family that sat next to us knew Jackie. The next day when I got on Facebook, one of my friends from college (who lives in Arkansas) posted a message on Jackie's Facebook page.

> Jackie is a living illustration of using the natural talents that the Lord has given her to grow the kingdom of God and love people. She is also a living illustration of the fact that it is never too late for someone to surrender to God's plan.

Jackie was raised by a single mom who tried her absolute best to make life happen every day for her family. Though her mom did all she could, Jackie did not grow up in a loving environment and was surrounded by anger and poverty.

Her family was an example of poverty in the United States, which is often overlooked, because it is different from poverty in a developing country. Jackie's family was not without running water; but they did have to wash their clothes in the sink, because the laundromat was just too expensive.

One day when Jackie was six years old, she was playing in the parking lot of her family's apartment complex and was lured away by a stranger. The man told her that he was going to catch bunnies in the woods and asked if she wanted to see them.

Jackie describes the subsequent abduction and abuse as the most terrifying experience of her life. She knew nothing about God and had never heard of Jesus; but as she trembled beside this man in the woods, she distinctly heard a whisper in her heart that simply said, "Run or die." Not until she was thirty-four did she realize that the whisper had been the voice of God.

Jackie ran and escaped possible death, but she did not escape the terrible aftermath that an abused child must endure. Her family did not have the money or resources to send Jackie for counseling or healing; that day was simply never spoken of again, and she was expected to move on. Jackie began to show textbook signs of a child who has been abused. She started having sex at the age of thirteen; and, when she went away to college, she became fully immersed in drugs, alcohol and partying.

Before Jackie met Corey (later to be her husband) she had slept with every guy at her university. Getting married and having children helped Jackie slow down her reckless behavior, but she and Corey also prided themselves on getting their boys to sleep through a good party. Their lifestyle of carefree living came to an abrupt stop, however, when Corey and Jackie found themselves on the brink of divorce and financially destitute.

In the meantime, Jackie's mom had married an incredible Christian man and had also become a Christian herself. When Jackie attended church with them, she heard truths like "Jesus loves you" and "God wants a relationship with you."

But she believed that these phrases were just crutches for people to hold onto, that there was no way they could be true—not for her anyway. Jesus would never love her if He knew everything about her.

Jackie and Corey's marriage went from bad to worse and reached a point where the only things left in their relationship were hate and anger. One night, during a particularly epic blowout on their front porch, Corey stopped arguing and broke down in tears. He told Jackie that he thought he was supposed to go inside and ask Jesus to be his Savior.

Jackie called her mom and stepdad because she wasn't sure what that meant or how to proceed; and, at the age of thirty, Corey and Jackie Hooks prayed together for the very first time, asking Jesus to save them from their mess and rescue them. Jackie calls it their road-to-Damascus experience. Though they had said "no" to God many times before, Jesus met them where they were, and this time they said "yes."

Jesus saved them from their sin and offered them eternal life, but it wasn't all rainbows and unicorns from then on. Corey was unemployed, and they had nothing. In a desperate search, Corey found a job in a suburb of Houston, and God soon moved the Hooks family to Katy, Texas. Soon after they arrived, Jackie surprisingly found out that she was pregnant with baby Hooks number four. This was a game changer, as they had expected Jackie to go back to work as a teacher to help out with finances. Jackie had tried to find a job, but no one wanted to hire someone who would soon go on maternity leave.

As she came to grips with an unplanned pregnancy and an uprooted plan, Jackie kept hearing about a new school located in the third ward of Houston called Generation One Academy. Generation One was a private Christian school designed to meet the unique environmental, sociological and educational needs of severely at-risk children.

After hearing about it enough times, Jackie knew that God was asking her to contact Generation One and schedule a tour. As she drove to the school, she thought that the Lord was going to ask her to apply for a job there, but that is not what the Lord had in mind—not at all. As Jackie walked through the campus, she was completely broken for the kids she saw. She relived her own feelings of being a vulnerable, at-risk child in poverty. When she asked the Lord why He had brought her there, His answer was simple: "Feed my sheep" (John 21:17). Jackie still thought this meant that she was to teach at the school—to help provide the kids with spiritual feeding—but that's not what the Lord meant.

That night at home, she got on her knees in prayer, trying to figure out what in the world God had meant by "feed my sheep."

That's when she remembered that the director of Generation One had said that the school was applying for a grant from the government to provide lunches for students who simply did not have the funds to pay for it out of pocket. Most of the kids did not even have a permanent residence, much less the ability to pack lunches. That's when one of the most defining rich-young-ruler moments of Jackie's life took place: Jesus was asking her if she would feed His sheep by providing lunches for the kids at Generation One.

She had no idea how she would do that; there was no way her family could fund lunches for sixty to seventy kids a day. She decided that before she said "yes" to Jesus, she would tell Corey about the idea.

She knew that he would say she was crazy, and out of submission to her husband, she would be off the hook on this lunch craziness! But Corey's response was, "Well, if God is asking you to do it, then you'd better do it."

So Jackie said "yes" to filling these kids' little bellies, despite the fact that she had no idea how to go about it. Later that week, as Jackie watched her boys at football practice, she told another mom what God was asking of her. As she explained how scared out of her mind she was trying to figure out how to make this happen (remember, Jackie is a connector, not an organizer), another mom overheard her. That mom, Jody Cook, picked up her chair and came and sat down by Jackie. God was about to use Jackie to make one of the most significant connections of her life. In the second conversation that Jackie had ever had with her, Jody outlined how the entire thing would happen. Within a few weeks, Jody created a menu for the entire semester and set up rosters for teams to pack lunches for the entire school and then transport them to Generation One. These teams would decorate each lunch sack, insert Scripture cards in every one and pray over each lunch by the child's name. It is an incredible ministry and one that my family has been part of for the last three years.

Jackie Hooks

As Jackie says, "There is nothing intimidating about serving Jesus by packing a lunch, but it sure is powerful. Anyone can pack a lunch." God used the first lunch, delivered on October 18, 2012, to birth an entire ministry called "Pruning Hooks," which allows every day, ordinary women to serve Jesus in extraordinary ways. Jackie would be the first to tell you it's not her, but Jesus working through her, and she is right.

Whether Jackie had said "yes" or "no," Jesus would have figured out a way to feed the kids at Generation One; but Jackie would have missed out on the ride and the blessings that have come from connecting women to so many needs in our community and watching them become the hands and feet of Jesus.

Today, Pruning Hooks not only delivers lunches to Generation One, but also ministers to families living temporarily in Houston due to the need for medical care for a loved one. They organize food and care packages for the homeless and recently started a program to train women in other cities how to begin a Pruning Hooks-type ministry in their areas.

Over the years, Pruning Hooks has provided baby supplies to teen moms and taken hotline calls from those being exploited and sexually trafficked. It has also provided prom dresses and organized prom events for teenagers suffering from illnesses that prevented them from attending their own high school proms.

Jackie teaches Bible studies at churches all over town. Once a month she leads Pruning Hooks nights, during which women have the opportunity to tell their stories and share how God works through them.

Jackie has not let her past determine her future. And because of that, God has used her to free so many people from the bondage of sin, complacency, greed, entitlement, poverty and hopelessness. Jackie looks like your ordinary stay-at-home mom living in the suburbs, but her surrendered heart to Jesus has resulted in anything but an ordinary life.

Ordinary People Can Do Extraordinary Things

The stories could continue on. In fact, I could write an entire book filled with stories of people I know who are courageously and boldly choosing to live a life of surrendered blessing by allowing God to take ownership.

I could tell you about my friend Andrea, who said "yes" to God when He asked her to host a handful of women once a month for dinner at her house to talk about Jesus, and how two years later her efforts have resulted in a dozen women across our city also hosting dinners and an annual conference for over 250 women. I could tell you about Dan Kiriny, who noticed a large homeless population in College Station while attending school at Texas

A&M University. And now, ten years later, Dan and his wife lead church services for the homeless every Saturday and Sunday followed by a meal in a local park. I could tell you about Jay and Heather Motley, who added to their family by adoption—giving their awesome biological daughter, McKayla, two ridiculously cute sisters from China, Amelia and Emma—and who continue to encourage and counsel others families to consider adopting internationally.

I could tell you about my friend Ashley, who, instead of allowing a newborn and a two-year-old to prevent her from ministering to those in our community, has joined several local playgroups and, as a result, has connected many families in our area to the local church and to Jesus. I could tell you about a special group of ladies who said "yes" to God when He asked them to boldly speak words of encouragement into the life of a friend, which resulted in the book that you are reading right now.

Each of these stories tells of ordinary people who acted on God-given convictions; as a result, the Lord did, and continues to do, extraordinary things through their lives. These people have baggage, just as you and I do, but they don't let their baggage define who God created them to be.

They have families just as you and I do, but they don't allow that to stop them from taking action; instead, they boldly live out their faith in front of their families. They have kids to raise, laundry to scrub, Christmas cards to send, dishes to wash, bills to pay and relationships to invest in—just as we all do! There is no difference between what God is doing through these people and what God wants to do through you and me. Let's not allow our fears to keep us from a surrendered heart and a new definition of blessing.

9

Is It Worth It?

So you've bought in. You have weeded through your social media accounts and deleted all the posts with #blessed. You have unapologetically been using descriptions like "meek," "poor in spirit" and "pure in heart" when giving advice to your friends, and you have no plans to stop anytime soon. You have clearly stated that you just want to hunger and thirst for righteousness. And when your four-year-old throws an epic fit on Christmas morning over not getting the $500 LEGO Star Wars ship that he wanted, you calmly tell him that this is the persecution that comes with living a blessed life.

Okay, maybe you aren't that extreme yet, but that's the picture I like to have in my mind when thinking about people reading this book. It makes me feel like you're "getting it."

Yet perhaps a question in the back of your mind continues to haunt you—one you would not dare say aloud much less ask someone, because, well, it's not very Christian. But it is a daunting question: *Is it worth it?* Is this life of blind, risky obedience really worth it? It's a hard question to admit having, because it feels as if we are almost asking if following Jesus is worth it—and, of course, we know that the answer is "yes."

But why? Why is the answer "yes"? The most obvious response is because Jesus gave His life for us so that we could have eternal life in the most perfect place ever, and the least we can do is hand over our lives and follow Him. Then why aren't we doing it? Why is it so hard?

Because, as we make intentional choices and sacrifices that naturally come with aligning our lives with God's Word instead of the culture around us, we experience times of doubt—times when we look around and see that everyone else's life seems so much easier than ours, and even a lot more fun. These are the times we find ourselves asking, *Is this even worth it?*

This is one of the most important questions that we need to wrestle with as Christ followers. When we are walking through seasons of doubt, and "faking it 'til we make it" just isn't working anymore, we need to be able to hold firm to the vision from the Lord as to why He desires us to live lives of true blessing.

Without a Vision, We Will Perish

Proverbs 29:18 says, "Where there is no vision, the people perish: but he that keepeth the law, happy is he" (KJV). This verse has been widely used to convince leaders that it is important for an organization to have a vision statement, and I agree with that. A vision statement for any organization is important; it communicates to the employees why they do what they do, and it communicates to the patrons the goal of the organization. But that is not the intended meaning behind this verse.

In this proverb, the word "vision" in Hebrew is *chazon*, and it refers to a prophetic word from the Lord, which many times was spoken through a prophet.[1] Thanks to Jesus, we don't have to depend on a prophet today to receive an inspired word from God; we have an entire book of inspired words.

So what this proverb is saying is that when our life is without inspiration from the Word of God, we will perish. In other words, the Word of God is what gives us vision for our lives—and holds us fast when we are tempted to wonder if our sacrifice is worth it.

The New International Version renders this verse, "Where there is no revelation, people cast off restraint; but blessed is the one who heeds wisdom's instruction."

When we live without revelation from God's Word, we have no compass to keep us on track, so we drift away from truth and make up our own standards. "But blessed" are those who adhere to God's Word and align their lives to it.

If it is essential for an organization to have a vision statement, how much more important is it that we know God's vision for our lives? God's vision, the Holy Bible, is what will keep us on track and prevent us from drifting away from truth and creating our own standards of living.

We need the vision of God's Word as we seek to live a truly blessed life, especially in those times when we, and others around us, ask, "Is it worth it?" This is a question we should be able to answer not only for ourselves for when the journey gets hard, but also because other people are watching us and asking the same question in regard to the choices we make.

Here are several reasons why it is absolutely worth it to redefine our understanding of "blessed"—and our entire lives—to follow Christ.

Why It's Worth It #1: Indescribable Joy

John Piper defines joy as "a good feeling in the soul, produced by the Holy Spirit, as he causes us to see the beauty of Christ in the Word and in the world."[2] I love how Piper points out who produces joy (the Holy Spirit) and then how it is produced (seeing the beauty of Christ in the Word and in the world).

We cannot produce true genuine joy, only the Holy Spirit can do that. But we sure can set ourselves up for the Holy Spirit to work in us by aligning our lives with Jesus' definition of blessing. This process starts by spending time in the Word and then doing what it says about building God's kingdom and loving people. In turn, seeing the beauty of Christ in the Word brings us joy.

When I asked Jackie Hooks (whose story is told in the previous chapter) how long her Pruning Hooks ministry had been in existence, I almost fell over when she said three years. Knowing the sheer number of people God has reached through this organization, I for sure thought that it was at least ten years old.

When I said, "What a crazy three years!" Jackie responded, "It has been—and it has been the best adventure of my life."

At the same time, having watched it grow over the past three years, I can tell you that it has not always been easy for Jackie, and I know she has thought at times, *What in the world have I gotten myself into? I should probably shut this whole thing down.*

Joy is not a by-product of ease. In fact, the most joyful things in my life have been the hardest things.

One of the greatest joys of my life is being mom to my four kids; but it is also, by far, the hardest thing I have ever done in my entire life. I am proud of my children every single day, but they bring me the most joy when I witness them making a decision *on their own* that brings glory to God. I can't produce that feeling of joy; but I can live my life in such a way that it points my kids to Christ and, in return, produces the feeling of joy when they make God-honoring decisions.

Those feelings of joy carry me through the really hard times of parenting—like when I have to discipline my kids—because I know that I am refining them, which will hopefully lead all of us toward more joy.

The Jones family children

When James wrote to the many Jewish Christians who had fled Israel because of persecution, he started off by saying, "Consider it pure joy, my brothers and sisters, whenever you face trials of many kinds, because you know that the testing of your faith produces perseverance" (James 1:2–3). In the same way, when we experience the true joy that comes from obedience in Christ, it makes our difficult trials worth it.

This was exactly Jesus' point in John 15:11 when He said, "I have told you this so that my joy may be in you and that your joy may be complete." Jesus was preparing His disciples for His death. So He was encouraging them that if they would abide in Him, they would experience the same joy that Jesus had experienced in His fellowship with the Father, and that this joy would carry Him through the suffering He was about to undergo.[3]

This promise holds true for us today. It feels incredibly selfish to say that one of the reasons that it is totally worth it to follow Jesus is the indescribable joy it brings us; but I am thankful for that joy, and I will receive it!

Why It's Worth It #2: Hope for a Weary World

I love baby Jesus as much as the next person, and I love to celebrate His birthday—we make a cake, sing "Happy Birthday" to Jesus, the whole thing—but I can't stand Christmas music. And the radio stations that play it 24/7 starting the day after Thanksgiving—no, I just can't.

So I was shocked when I found myself in tears while singing "O Holy Night" this past year during one of our church's Christmas Eve candlelight services. I don't know if it was the hot wax running down my hand due to the useless flimsy wax guard or the fact that I am in my thirties now (and apparently emotions are harder to control when you are in your thirties). But when we got to "a thrill of hope, the weary world rejoices," it was as if all of a sudden I finally understood the fulfillment of each and every promise that Jesus' birth represented, and I could not stop the tears from flowing.

That line hit me like a ton of bricks, because for the first time in my life I felt as if I was living in a world that could relate to the environment in which Jesus had been born. I have never been more burdened for our world than I have been recently. Our world is full of mass shootings, slavery, religious hatred, child sex trafficking, orphans, identity crises, prostitution, broken families, homelessness, drug addictions, sex addictions, and addictions I don't even know about—without Jesus it is hopeless and bleak. This weary world desperately needs a thrill of hope, and we have it.

We know the answer for attaining real hope in a world in which people are trying to fill their lives with anything that will offer some sort of hope, even if it is temporary. We know the only One who offers authentic hope! Our faith isn't just about us—it's first about bringing glory to God, and second about building His kingdom by loving others. From the time Adam took a bite of that fruit in the Garden of Eden, humanity has been in need of a Savior, and our world today is no exception.

But in our efforts to explain to people that God desires to be more than a checklist of rules, that He wants a personal relationship with us, we have created a myth that our faith is *merely* personal.

As with any myth, it contains an element of truth that has been distorted. See, my relationship with Christ is personal in the same way that my marriage is personal. Some aspects of my marriage are shared only between my husband and I, and those parts are not for the rest of the world or even our best of friends.

But if I never talk to others about my husband or our relationship, if I never serve him or prioritize him over others, I'm not sure that other people will be driven toward a better marriage because of our union. In fact, most people won't even know that we are married, much less in love. Some aspects of my marriage very much need to be lived out in front of other people—our kids, our friends, our neighbors—to set an example for them.

Our relationship with Christ is the same way. Now this doesn't justify an "in your face" type of faith, but this weary world needs to see the hope of Jesus Christ. Peter so beautifully describes this hope: "Praise be to the God and Father of our Lord Jesus Christ! In his great mercy he has given us new birth into a living hope through the resurrection of Jesus Christ from the dead, and into an inheritance that can never perish, spoil or fade" (1 Pet. 1:3–4).

Because of Christ's death on the cross, we are given new life and a new living hope for our future, and we become a living illustration of going from death to life! Now this is not a message that we should keep under wraps; we should be shouting it from the rooftops! This is a hope that we need to communicate not only in our words, but in our actions as well.

That's a huge responsibility, because just as our words and actions can drive others toward Christ, they can also drive them away, so we have to proceed with great dependence on the Holy Spirit. The point is, we have to proceed, because *our faith isn't just about us*.

This is a thrill of hope that for sure will cause a weary world to rejoice! We never know how God is going to use our faithfulness in following Christ in someone else's life. If we knew for certain that the sacrifices, persecution and difficult times that come with following Christ would be instrumental in one day leading our kids, our spouse, our friends—or even people we have never met—to a closer relationship with Jesus, wouldn't it be worth it? Wouldn't we give up everything else to do it?

Why It's Worth It #3: We Are Not of This World

If I could sum up this entire book in just a few verses, these two would win every time: "Our light and momentary troubles are achieving for us an eternal glory that far outweighs them all.

So we fix our eyes not on what is seen, but on what is unseen, since what is seen is temporary, but what is unseen is eternal" (2 Cor. 4:17–18).

If we could take a peek behind the curtain to see the unseen, even for just a second, we wouldn't ask whether saying "yes" to Jesus is worth it. The question wouldn't even enter our minds, because the glory of heaven would be so overwhelming. The problem is that we can't see to the other side of eternity. At times we get glimpses of it as we follow Christ, but even the most fulfilling day of our lives cannot come remotely close to just one minute in heaven, much less an eternity.

The Western world has many times been compared to that of the Corinthians. Though Christian persecution did exist in Corinth, it was much less severe than in other cities—to the point that Paul stayed in Corinth for a year and a half (a long stint for Paul), because he simply was not concerned for his life.

The city of Corinth has been described as intellectually alert, materially prosperous, culturally varied and religiously diverse. In other words, Corinth consisted of a bunch of wealthy intellectuals who had money to burn and time to do it. Does that sound familiar? These people were Gentiles, so they were not particularly fond of the Jewish Paul. Many attacked his character and even his physical appearance. During Paul's time in Corinth, he saw firsthand that the pursuit of the things of this world over the pursuit of God was a problem for the Corinthians, and Paul felt that they needed to be reminded of what was actually important. I feel that Paul would have the same message for Americans if he was writing a letter to us today.

The ability to set our eyes on "things unseen" doesn't mean that we won't ever experience sadness or disappointment; it just means that we understand that what happens here on earth isn't the endgame. I have, unfortunately, had many friends walk through the unbearable pain of losing a child.

One friend, Jamie, lost her daughter in a car accident caused by a drunk driver; it was sudden, unexpected and incredibly painful. Cara was a senior in high school when it happened and had devoted her life to serving Christ and others. She had countless journal entries and social media posts about wanting to spend her life making God famous, and everyone would agree that she did just that. Jamie said multiple times that the one thing that brought her comfort in such unimaginable tragedy was the fact that because Cara had loved the Lord with her whole being, she was now spending eternity with the Father, and they would one day be reunited again.

Jamie was still crushed and brokenhearted by the reality that her daughter was no longer with her, but her hope was renewed because of the promise of eternity. She chose to set her eyes on things unseen.

If I could ask Cara if it was worth it—if saying "no" to things here on earth in order to follow Jesus was worth it—I have no doubt in my mind that she would give a resounding "yes" a thousand times over.

The fact that we cannot see what lies on the other side of eternity is, at times, both to our detriment and our benefit. The challenge for us is figuring out *how* to set our eyes on things unseen. The best and only way to do it is to live a life that prioritizes the things that are dear to the heart of the Lord—building His kingdom and loving people.

My Family's Newest Rich-Young-Ruler Moment

For the past two years, my family has fought relentlessly to tear down the American dream in our lives and to ask God what kind of dream He wants for our family. Through many hours spent on our knees, we finally told God that He had our "yes," whatever His calling might be, before He even asks the question. And wouldn't you know it, He recently presented us with another rich-young-ruler moment.

The Lord began painting a picture in our hearts of a community of people that found true sustaining hope in Jesus Christ and then gave it to the world around them—a place that intentionally built bridges between those of different ethnicities, socioeconomic statuses, seasons of life and even religious views; a place that used the Bible to engage our society in a relevant and loving way and where people actively fought the injustices of this world, both locally and internationally.

God showed us an organization that, as Andy Stanley says, showed people they mattered to God, even if God didn't matter to them, a church that equipped and challenged its congregation to live against the grain of the American dream and embrace radical generosity.

At the time the Lord began piecing this together, I was coming up on my nine-year anniversary of being on staff at the church where I worked. I loved the church deeply; I had seen it grow from 150 to 3,000 people and been constantly overwhelmed by the opportunities that the Lord had given me during my time there. I had built some clout among the people and the staff, I was well paid, and for the most part I got to do whatever I wanted within the bounds of the vision of the church. Our pastor had known me since I was twelve years old. He had led me to Christ, baptized me, married my husband and me, visited me in the hospital for the births of our three biological children, and come to our house when we brought our fourth child home from China.

He had hired me, at the ridiculous age of twenty-three, to run and lead an entire department. At the time, I thought I was super mature and so ready for the job, but looking back now I realize how big a risk he took by hiring a mere baby. As the gravity of what the Lord was asking of my family became clearer, my heart grew heavy from the reality of what it would mean: leaving a place where my family was deeply loved and I had spent my entire career.

Even as the Lord worked in our hearts to lead us to a new church, my first thought was not that we would plant a church, because that sounded super scary (since 80 percent of all church plants fail in the first year). But one day, in my prayer time, I asked the Lord, "Okay, God, I know that You are calling us to something new, but where?"

That same day I was reading in the book of Acts, studying the New Testament church, and I came across this: "Keep watch over yourselves and all the flock of which the Holy Spirit has made you overseers. Be shepherds of the church of God, which he bought with his own blood" (20:28). I still get chills when I think about this moment.

"What do you want me to do with this?" I asked the Lord. "I placed you in the fastest-growing area in the United States for a reason," He showed me. "There are too many people and not enough churches. I gave you a vision to be part of a new church—now go and be a shepherd who is concerned for *all* those living in your community, whom my Son gave His life for." "I'm sorry, what? I don't think I can do that." "You can't, but I can do it through you. You just have to decide if you are going to be obedient or not."

I was in the midst of studying the rich young ruler, and I thought I was studying from the perspective of already having said "yes" to my rich-young-ruler moments. Little did I know that the Lord had been preparing my family for what was by far the scariest rich-young-ruler moment we had experienced up until this point. (I say "up until this point," because I now know better than to think that this one will be our last.)

God has always been faithful to surround Chad and me with amazing couples who listen to us, pray with us and give us wise, godly advice when we need it. One of those couples is Ryan and Ashley Lokkesmoe.

Ryan is a pastor who has a doctorate in biblical studies. And if you think that is impressive, you should meet his wife Ashley; she is definitely the more impressive of the two. She is kind, levelheaded, and looks for ways to connect with those who don't know Jesus in all seasons of her life.

As Chad and I shared with Ryan and Ashley about what we felt the Lord was calling us to do and asked them to pray for us to have clarity, discernment and boldness, they began to share with us that the Lord had been working on their hearts in the same way with some of the same convictions. I was left thinking, *Lord, what in the world are You doing?*

After several more conversations over the next few weeks, the four of us decided that we would take a month to pray and fast, asking for definite direction from the Lord. I already had an idea of what the Lord was going to say because of what God had shown me in my earlier prayer times, but the idea of planting a church was a new concept for Ryan and Ashley and for sure not something that we had prayed about all together.

And, despite what the Lord had shown me about being "shepherds of the church of God," I had still not directly asked Him if He was really asking us to plant a church, mostly because I was terrified of actually saying the words aloud. So on July 1, 2015, I asked the Lord for the first time, "God, are You asking us to plant a church?"

His response was simple: "Yes. That is what I have been preparing you for."

At the end of a month of prayer and fasting, Chad and I scheduled dinner with Ryan and Ashley. And on the evening of August 7, 2015, Real Hope Community Church was born. Since that day, our lives have been a roller coaster of excitement, fear, hope, insecurity and thankfulness. We don't know how things will turn out, but one thing we know for sure: we wouldn't trade this life of Jesus-defined blessing for anything on earth!

Living in Light of Eternity

The key to living a boldly blessed life is simple—we can't let anything get in the way of what God wants to do through us. None of us wants to get to the end of our lives and wish that we had taken more risks for God or lived more in the moment. We should live in the constant reality of James 4:14: "You do not even know what will happen tomorrow. What is your life? You are a mist that appears for a little while and then vanishes." In light of how quickly our lives go by, nothing except glorifying God with all that we are seems important.

In the grand scheme of time, our lives are just small dots on the spectrum of eternity. I don't want to take up even one day pursuing the stuff of this world, because it could all be gone at any second.

I want to spend my days pouring into things that will far outlast this life—building God's kingdom and loving people. This journey that the Lord calls us to is not easy, and few will choose it. But that's why Jesus said, "Enter through the narrow gate. For wide is the gate and broad is the road that leads to destruction, and many enter through it. But small is the gate and narrow the road that leads to life, and only a few find it" (Matt. 7:13–14). But it's worth it. It's more than worth it.

Be one of the few who enter through the narrow gate. Don't be too blessed to say "yes!"

Notes

Chapter 1: When Did Christianity Get So Boring?

1. For clarification of the author's meaning of American dream, please refer to chapter 2, "How the American Dream Has Distorted the Gospel." See also chapter 2, note 2.

Chapter 2: But Your Love Doesn't Pay My Bills

1. Berry Gordy Jr. and Janie Bradford, "Money (That's What I Want)," single by Barrett Strong, Anna Records, 1959, 45 rpm.
2. *Dictionary.com*, s.v. "American Dream," accessed February 25, 2016, http://www.dictionary.com/browse/american-dream.
3. Justin Myers, Anu Narayanswamy and Soo Oh, "How America Gives," *The Chronicle of Philanthropy*, last updated January 5, 2015, https://philanthropy.com/interactives/how-america-gives#search.
4. "Top 10 Fastest Growing ZIP Codes," *fine lines: The Maponics Blog*, March 13, 2014, http://www.maponics.com/blog/2014/03/13/top-10-fastest-growing-zip-codes.
5. Mike Holmes, "What Would Happen If the Church Tithed?" *Relevant*, last updated March 8, 2016, http://www.relevantmagazine.com/god/church/what-would-happen-if-church-tithed.

6. Mark D. Taylor, "How Much Was the Widow's Mite," *NLT* (blog), April 19, 2010, http://www.nltblog.com/index.php/2010/04/how-much-was-the-widows-mite.
7. Mark Batterson, Twitter, August 24, 2013, https://twitter.com/markbatterson/status/371261427907981312.
8. "Volkswagen Used Car Ad: Keeping Up with the Joneses," YouTube, accessed February 25, 2016, https://www.youtube.com/watch?v=hJVqCilYd0w.
9. "What Percentage of the World's Population Own a Car?" Answers, accessed March 29, 2016, http://www.answers.com/Q/What_percentage_of_the_world%27s_population_own_a_car.
10. Erin El Issa, "2015 American Household Credit Card Debt Study," NerdWallet (blog), November 2–4, 2015, https://www.nerdwallet.com/blog/credit-card-data/average-credit-card-debt-household.
11. "Sarah McLachlan SPCA Commercial," YouTube, accessed February 25, 2016, https://www.youtube.com/watch?v=IO9d2PpP7tQ.
12. I think it's important to distinguish between absolute poverty–a condition characterized by severe deprivation of basic human needs, including food and shelter–and relative poverty (or income inequality), which can be viewed as those whose income level falls below the average income of an area.

Chapter 3: Blessed Are the Empty

1. Allen Ross, "7. The Beatitudes (Matthew 5:1–12)," from the series An Exposition of the Gospel of Matthew, Bible.org, March 17, 2006, https://bible.org/seriespage/7-beatitudes-matthew-51-12.

2. *Dictionary.com*, s.v. "meek," accessed June 21, 2016, http://www.dictionary.com/browse/meek?s=t.
3. John Piper, "Blessed Are the Meek," Desiring God, February 9, 1986, http://www.desiringgod.org/messages/blessed-are-the-meek.
4. Love146 fights against child trafficking, starting at the grassroots level, through prevention education in US school districts and by mobilizing volunteer task forces to educate community members (medical personnel, hotel management staff, gas station attendants, etc.) about the red flags to look for in a trafficking situation. The organization lobbies for changes in US legislation to create more severe penalties for those caught exploiting children (currently the penalty for trafficking drugs in America is more severe than the penalty for trafficking children) and to help vulnerable kids in foster care. When learning about Love146, many people ask, "Why don't you just raise funds to buy these kids out of trafficking?" Though that sounds like an easy solution, it is not the most effective means of ending child trafficking, because it only gives the industry more funds to purchase more children. For more information about Love146 and combating child trafficking, go to https://love146.org.
5. "Child Trafficking," UNICEF, accessed March 3, 2016, https://www.unicefusa.org/mission/protect/trafficking.
6. Rob Morris, "Why 146?" Love146, accessed March 1, 2016, https://love146.org/love-story.

Chapter 4: For They Will Be Filled

1. Andy Stanley, "Andy Stanley Quotes," Twitter, November 25, 2015, https://twitter.com/stanleyquotes/

status/669568187483181056.

2. Eugene H. Merrill, "Fast, Fasting," *Baker's Evangelical Dictionary of Biblical Theology*, accessed March 29, 2016, http://www.biblestudytools.com/dictionary/fast-fasting/.
3. For more information about fasting, read Richard J. Foster, *Celebration of Discipline: The Path to Spiritual Growth* (San Francisco: Harper, 1993).
4. "Myths About Homelessness," Portland Rescue Mission, accessed March 3, 2016, http://www.portlandrescuemission.org/learn-more/myths-about-homelessness.
5. Ross, "The Beatitudes (Matthew 5:1–12)."
6. "Word Counts: How Many Times Does a Word Appear in the Bible?" Christian Bible Reference Site, accessed March 3, 2016, http://www.christianbiblereference.org/faq_WordCount.htm.

Chapter 5: A Higher Standard

1. John Piper, "Blessed Are the Peacemakers," *Desiring God*, March 9, 1986, http://www.desiringgod.org/messages/blessed-are-the-peacemakers.
2. Brett Tarbell, "Beaten for Jesus," *Stories of Persecution* (blog), Open Doors, August 14, 2015, https://www.opendoorsusa.org/christian-persecution/stories/tag-blog-post/beaten-for-jesus.
3. For more info about these martyrs, please see: Patrick J. Kiger, "How Did the Apostles Die?" National Geographic Channel, February 19, 2015, http://channel.nationalgeographic.com/killing-jesus/articles/how-did-the-apostles-die/; "William Tyndale–Burned for Translating the Bible into English," Awesome Stories, accessed April 28, 2016, https://www.awesomestories.com/asset/view/

William-Tyndale-Burned-for-Translating-the-Bible-into-English; "Dietrich Bonhoeffer, German Theologian and Resister," *Christianity Today*, accessed April 28, 2016, http://www.christianitytoday.com/history/people/martyrs/dietrich-bonhoeffer.html; "Jim Elliott: No Fool," Christianity.com, accessed April 28, 2016, http://www.christianity.com/church/church-history/church-history-for-kids/jim-elliot-no-fool-11634862.html.

4. C.S. Lewis, *Mere Christianity* (New York: Macmillan, 1960), 120.

Chapter 6: Moment of Truth

1. Billy Sunday, "Billy Sunday Quotes," Goodreads, accessed April 28, 2016, https://www.goodreads.com/author/quotes/2319780.Billy_Sunday.
2. Jen Hatmaker, *For the Love: Fighting for Grace in a World of Impossible Standards* (Nashville: Thomas Nelson, 2015), 18.

Chapter 7: Two Men Who Said Yes

1. *Hitchcock's Bible Names Dictionary*, s.v. Sanhedrin, Bible Study Tools, accessed March 3, 2016, http://www.biblestudytools.com/dictionary/sanhedrin.
2. "Zacchaeus," lyricsofsongs.net, accessed July 11, 2016, http://lyricsofsongs.net/a/289-action-bible-songs-cedarmont-kids/1331-zacchaeus.html.
3. Keith Stump, "Digging Up the Bible," Grace Communion International, 1995, accessed April 29, 2016, https://www.gci.org/bible/digging.
4. Clement of Alexandria, *Stromata* 4.6.35.2, Early Christian Writings, accessed April 29, 2016, http://www.earlychristianwritings.com/text/traditionsmatthias.html.

5. Brian Haughton, "What Happened to the Great Library at Alexandria?" *Ancient History Encyclopedia*, February 1, 2011, http://www.ancient.eu/article/207.

Chapter 8: I'm Just Ordinary—What Can I Do for God?

1. Pediacities NYC, s.v. "East Harlem,"accessed August 25, 2016, http://nyc.pediacities.com/Resource/Neighborhood/East_Harlem.
2. NYC Health, s.v. "Community Health Profiles"accessed August 25, 2016, https://www1.nyc.gov/assets/doh/downloads/pdf/data/2006chp-303.pdf.

Chapter 9: Is It Worth It?

1. Bible Hub (Commentaries), s.v. "Proverbs 29:18," *Pulpit Commentary*, accessed March 3, 2016, http://biblehub.com/commentaries/proverbs/29-18.htm.
2. John Piper, "How Do You Define Joy?" Desiring God, July 25, 2015, http://www.desiringgod.org/articles/how-do-you-define-joy.
3. Bible Hub (Commentaries), s.v. "John 15:11," *Cambridge Bible for Schools and Colleges*, accessed March 3, 2016, http://biblehub.com/commentaries/john/15-11.htm.

PUBLICATIONS
Fort Washington, PA 19034

This book is published by CLC Publications, an outreach of CLC Ministries International. The purpose of CLC is to make evangelical Christian literature available to all nations so that people may come to faith and maturity in the Lord Jesus Christ. We hope this book has been life changing and has enriched your walk with God through the work of the Holy Spirit. If you would like to know more about CLC, we invite you to visit our website:
www.clcusa.org

To know more about the remarkable story of the founding of CLC International we encourage you to read

LEAP OF FAITH

Norman Grubb

Paperback
Size $5\frac{1}{4}$ x 8, Pages 248
ISBN: 978-0-87508-650-7
ISBN (*e-book*): 978-1-61958-055-8

THE UNFAIR ADVANTAGE

Dr. Harold L. Arnold, Jr.

Harold L. Arnold Jr. offers a fresh perspective on Christian marriages. Based on Second Peter 1, *The Unfair Advantage* explores the lives of couples with a deep level of marital intimacy that gives them an "unfair advantage." This advantage is rooted in faith-filled habits of martial stewardship, the Holy Spirit and grace.

Paperback
Size $5\frac{1}{4}$ x 8, Pages 186
ISBN: 978-1-61958-232-3
ISBN (*e-book*): 978-1-61958-233-0

FAITH THAT LASTS

Jon Nielson

In a society where many young adults flee the church, Jon Nielson helps parents raise their children with a Christian faith that does not fade with time. Through practical advice and five biblically based principles, Nielson provides guidance for the church, parents at every stage, and especially parents of children who have left the church.

Paperback
Size $5^{1}/_{4}$ x 8, Pages 251
ISBN: 978-1-61958-230-9
ISBN (*e-book*): 978-1-61958-231-6